BRONX

MEMOIR

PROJECT

VOLUME

1

Published by the Bronx Council on the Arts for BCA Media

Sign up for our newsletter at:
www.bronxarts.org

Contact: bronxwriters@bronxarts.org

Cover photo by Daisy Arroyo

Edited and designed by Charlie Vázquez and Kim Vaquedano

ISBN: 978-1500674069

ACKNOWLEDGMENTS

The *Bronx Memoir Project – Volume 1* book was made possible with major funding from the National Endowment for the Arts, NEA. The Bronx Council on the Arts is grateful for additional project support from the NYC Department of Cultural Affairs, NYS Council on the Arts, the Lambent Foundation Fund of the Tides Foundation, The Joan Mitchell Foundation, Lily Auchincloss Foundation, Inc., Councilman James Vacca, and the Bronx Delegation of the City Council.

The Bronx Memoir Project launched with a series of twenty-five free memoir writing workshops created by the Bronx Writers Center in spring of 2014, facilitated by a variety of BRIO literary arts winners, as well as celebrated fiction writers, memoirists, and poets.

The resulting works that were submitted via email to the editor became this first volume of previously untold, and almost entirely, unpublished stories.

A special gesture of gratitude goes to Jon Lewis Katz, Lauren Jost, Patricia O'Hanlon, Orlando Ferrand, Vanessa Mártir, Alicia Anabel Santos, Rich Villar, Alex Simmons, and Urayoán Noel for creating the wonderful workshops that created all of this work.

And also to our hosting organizations: the New York Public Library's Bronx Library Center, as well as the Kingsbridge and Melrose branches, the Poe Park Visitor Center, Mind Builders, The Bronx Documentary Center and The Point.

EXECUTIVE DIRECTOR INTRODUCTION

Stories are always best when told firsthand. This collection of memoir by Bronxites is no different in that regard. What does make a difference is this extraordinary first book that embraces the lives of a cross-generational collective of Bronx residents who bravely joined together to share and explore. It gives life to both the past and our present. The Bronx Memoir Project became the source of powerful work and writing.

We are delighted to be able to present this first volume—the fruit of noble labor.

The people of the Bronx have grown used to other folks talking about us, defining who we are and how we're living. It's time we tell our own stories, define ourselves and bring the people—their power and energy—into the light. Within these pages are just some of the voices of our borough—poignant, resolute and resilient.

Deirdre Scott
Executive Director
Bronx Council on the Arts
November 2014

EDITOR FOREWORD

As a Bronx native gone away and returned after 17 years in Oregon, California, and Baja Mexico, I've (yet again) fallen in love with my hometown and find myself defending it whenever I go elsewhere—a place where hardworking people live and love, a place of sensual and international beauty.

The Bronx Memoir Project was created as a means for Bronxites—born here or otherwise—to share their life stories. As editor I merely proofed and did not alter what arrived via email, after meeting with writers and workshop facilitators at the 25 free memoir writing workshops the Bronx Writers Center launched in various neighborhoods in spring 2014.

What I received was a roller-coaster ride of riveting tales, some shocking, others revealing and even heartbreaking—a mosaic of colors and textures that only a place as dynamic as the Bronx could produce.

I hope you enjoy reading them as much as I did, as I watched them grow from writing prompts, critiques, discussions, and first-draft attempts into a book. Let us hear the citizens of our borough share their stories for everyone's pleasure.

Charlie Vázquez
Director, Bronx Writers Center
October, 2014

BRONX

MEMOIR

PROJECT

VOLUME

1

TABLE OF CONTENTS

Meditation

Barbara Nahmias

I am alone, about to enter the tenement hallway of the building I lived in from age two to age fourteen, on Mosholu Parkway near Jerome Avenue in the Norwood section of the Bronx. I am about seven years old. There are two large glass outer doors to the building. I have the key that will unlock them, hanging around my neck on a dingy white cord.

As I come into the inner corridor, I begin to feel a sense of dread. The hallway is dank and dingy, with only dim light filtering in through a filthy window on the narrow stairwell landing. Just then, I am startled by the loud rumbling of the elevated subway train. You'd think I'd be used to it by now—that snake-like, seemingly living creature that roars through the neighborhood every ten minutes, day and night, rattling our windows and blocking out all conversation.

My mother has instructed me to go straight home from school and ring the doorbell of the old lady who lives next door to us. The lady will watch me until my mother gets home from work. I wish my baby sister were with me, but she is with another neighbor who did not want to take the two of us.

I ring the bell, my heart pounding, as it does each day when I stand here at the threshold. She takes a long time to come to the door. I begin to wonder if she has heard the bell because I know she is hard of hearing. While I stand there deciding whether to ring again, I hear the shuffling of her slippers, followed by the sound of two locks being unlatched.

The door finally opens. She says hello and motions me in, where a straight-backed wooden chair awaits me. The old woman asks if I would like a piece of fruit or a glass of milk. I refuse both. I won't eat anything in this place, which smells of mothballs and kitchen grease. I try not to move and pray that I don't have to use the bathroom. I try not to breathe too loud. I try to make myself invisible.

The old lady goes about her business, shuffling around slowly, doing things in the kitchen, humming a strange little sing-song tune over and over. The windows, which overlook the park, are wide open, but no breeze moves through them, just the shouts of the boys playing stickball and the rhyming songs of the girls jumping rope.

I sit in the straight-back chair for two-and-a-half hours, as I do every day, focusing on one thought and one thought only—the moment my mother will walk through the door to claim me. I had no clue then, but I realize now that this was the beginning of my meditation practice, and this is what would enable me to survive the years of neglect and loneliness I would experience for the rest of my childhood, my teenage years, and as a young adult.

On a Bronx Rooftop Long Ago

George Colón

Went by my old South Bronx neighborhood the other day. And stopping in front of my old building on Fox Street between Longwood and Intervale, I stared at eight windows lining the façade where mostly illegal Mexicans and Dominicans that now call these eight apartments home look out of those windows. Gone are Jewish neighbors of long ago, fleeing to the suburbs in their latest diaspora, later, replaced by Puerto Rican relatives and friends now residing in Saint Raymond's Cemetery.

I summoned two, like Jesus did Lazarus. They nearly took me with them to an early tomb. Up on the roof, fresh from their graves, they appear, raised by my literary powers, and yell down.

"Come on up, Papo."

I jump up the stoop's four steps and run up. Still kids at the end of the 50s, we fly kites, fling water-filled balloons down at people below and laugh. Indio, dark with round nose, mischievous black eyes and straight black hair that hearkens back to our Taíno Indian roots, takes out a pack of Marlboros stolen from their father. His brother Chino, white with the long, straight nose of our Spanish ancestors and wiry hair of our African forebears, lights one up. He inhales a lungful of smoke, holds it awhile, then exhales. Gives it to Indio who does the same, before turning it over to me.

I hesitate.

"Go ahead, puff, Papo," says Chino. "You a faggot if you don't."

I take my first drag and cough. They laugh. The 1960s come and they're jumping from roof to roof. First Chino hops the parapet and jumps, then Indio.

"You a faggot if you don't jump. Hang with us. We'll get you girls," they say.

I study wide eyed the long gap between buildings and the long drop below. They're thin and agile. I'm fat and clumsy. Will I do this? I want a girl. Just one. I see Jesus, too, down from the cross, wounds healed, walking the Earth again—

no, walking up on that roof. The devil shows up also, always around these parts, needing no invitation.

We're now in the desert, high up on that mountain during those forty days when Satan also prods.

"I'll give you great riches and domain over the continents. Follow me."

Indio and Chino graduate again. "Fire this zip gun. You a faggot if you don't."

Will I do it? Now it's the late 60s.

"Shoot up heroin," Chino says. "You'll feel real nice. You a faggot if you don't."

Will I?

After my Bronx elementary, intermediate and secondary educations, it was off to the State University, College at Oswego, fleeing the figurative flames of social unrest that in turn lit literal fires devastating my borough. I began my second life as a social science major and studied the sociology I expected would give me the necessary understanding of humans in society.

I'd acquired a social conscience during the 1960s Age of Aquarius, and a messianic complex that drove me to serve my people, a Puerto Rican Moses. In the crazy Age of Aquarius, I'd switched majors. English and American literature proving more appetizing than dry sociology, which failed to nourish me after I realized the futility of studying humanity, as one would animals in a lab. Rather, I fed on literature, which offered, in fewer words, a lot more insight into humanity's plight. The social sciences used many words to say very little.

I always looked up Chino and Indio during summers back home in the South Bronx.

"Don't know what you got against pot," Indio often said.

"Those strung-out addicts out there," I always answered, with a jerk of my thumb to the street below. "I won't end up like them."

My Hunts Point neighborhood had the highest density of drug addicts in the world then—after the communists had shot all the opium smokers in China.

"You won't," he said, flashing a smile, exposing a gold tooth. He donned one of those flashy knit sweaters that matched not just his expensive Brook Brothers pants, but his alligator shoes as well.

"Yeah, it's nice, real nice, bro. Those white college kids like it. You could do all right for yourself if we was to go into business and you sold to those blanquitos up there."

Would I? In my ragged jeans and sweatshirts, I'm tempted.

The 1970s came.

After college, I worked in anti-poverty programs for a while, but soon the Moses in me came down from the mountaintop to walk the realities of ground level, discovering my people didn't necessarily want to leave the desert and enter the Promised Land.

Still visited Indio in his Grand Concourse apartment, with lush rugs and wall-to-wall mirrors that rivaled Versailles. Went to parties there attended by well-dressed Italians in five-hundred dollar suits packing pistols, beautiful women at their side.

No, they were not Dante, Galileo, or da Vinci.

Then I became a teacher for the next thirty years.

By the way, Jesus refuses the Devil's enticements, unlike Adam and Eve. Now I don't believe everything those good Irish priests taught me in St. Athanasius a block away. But I still honor those Hebrew prophets who warn against stupid things, like living by the sword.

Did Jesus really rise? Is he really coming back?

Not sure. But he's still my guy. I refused, too. Ah, Ah. I'm a heterosexual male with balls screwed on tight, although I no longer harbor any prejudices against gay people.

I don't jump from roof to roof. Don't shoot that zip gun. Don't shoot heroin up these veins. Don't sell drugs.

Indio lives by the gun and falls through the precipice. Busted with cocaine—lots of cocaine—he does jail time and later the mob guns him down after he rats in exchange for a shorter prison term.

Jesus never packed a sword. I never packed a gun. Chino lives for the syringe and succumbs to AIDS. Too much heroin with unclean needles shared with too many junkies.

Back into their graves I send them.

Me, I'm still here, still in the Bronx, though I've moved on—and away from there.

Chevrolet

Ed Friedman

"Is it far?" I asked.

"No," my mother said, "you won't get carsick."

I had determined at the wise old age of seven that sitting in the back of the family car and going for extended trips was nausea inducing. While I sought to avoid these jaunts whenever possible, that Sunday's trip was unavoidable. My father, mother, four-year-old sister and I were off to the Chevrolet dealership.

My father was buying a new car.

I had zero interest in this adventure. My preference was to stay at home, on my street, navigating the uneven topography of the black and gray asphalt while trying to hit a small pink ball with a broomstick. While this may sound like a reality show contest, it was run-of-the mill Bronx stickball.

That Sunday, however, I was relegated to tolerating my younger sibling on our family adventure. I amused myself by reading the white and green highway signs as they whizzed past, wondering who Major Deegan was, and why an expressway was named after him.

True to my mother's word we were at the dealership in short order. A large oatmeal-colored building with blue lettering that spelled out CHEVROLET, seemed to be mostly windows, displaying shiny new cars, mostly red or black, with some two-toned models as well.

While my parents were immediately engaged by a salesman, my sister Renee and I, knowing our jobs as bored children, fidgeted to the annoyed distraction of the adults. The salesman, not wanting his prospective buyers distracted, called my sister and me over to his desk.

"I'm sure your parents won't mind if you play with these outside."

He then handed each of us a red and blue yoyo with CHEVROLET written in gold across both sides. My parents took the bait and shooed us outside to play with our new toys. Renee and I were both pretty happy as we had zero expectations for that trip.

We played with our yoyos in our own way. She seemed content to roll hers along the sidewalk while I attempted the tricks I'd seen on television. Watching me trying to manipulate my yoyo, Renee began to imitate what I was doing, however unsuccessfully. She, however had more tolerance for frustration than I, so she did not copy me when, annoyed by not being able to get the yoyo to do any of the things I'd seen it do on television, decided to hold the end of the string and whip the red and blue disc over my head as fast as I could.

I was fascinated by how the yoyo's color seemed to change as I whipped it around. I lost my grip on the string. The next sound I (and everyone else) heard was the shattering of a twenty-foot picture window. The red carpeting in the showroom looked like a showcase for diamonds, with small pieces of glass everywhere.

My parents and the salesman came running, accompanied by Renee's crying. I don't think she knew why she was crying except she knew something was very wrong.

Once we were deemed to be unharmed, my parents hustled us into the family car. My father, red-faced, and as mad as I had ever seen him, told us to sit, shut up, and wait for them.

He came back and added, "And you're not getting the yoyo back!"

Polio, Mothers and World War Two

Ersilia Crawford

Rome, 1939 - The fever was gone, and so too, the terrible pain. Polio had left me unable to use my right arm, luckily only that. Mother and us five daughters (in descending order): Marina, Clara, Ersilia (me), Giovanna and Luigina, were living in a very beautiful apartment on the Aventino, one of the Seven Hills of Rome.

Italy had just entered World War Two on the side of the Axis, with Germany and Japan. Father was in the U.S. on business, but being an enemy naval officer, was detained and later spent a few years in internment camps. Grandmother Ersilia came to Rome from Portici, Naples to help decide how to help me heal.

She suggested we visit a children's polio rehab and we went. I knew something about institutions and was petrified that grandmother could influence mother into leaving me there...and yes she loved the place. Mother looked at me, questioning. Without saying a word I looked at her with such intensity that she turned to her mother and said "No".

I would not be placed there. The bond between mother and I was so very special and remained so. Although she died in 1985, I always feel her by my side.

Portici, Naples, 1941 - I stood near the window in my grandmother's living room. It opened onto a narrow balcony overlooking the courtyard, with a palm tree near the fountain next to the perimeter wall. The sky was a clear blue, all was quiet.

My right arm was beginning to follow orders and move. The immersion in the hot black sand on the beach and in the hot wine dregs piled high against the wall of a neighbor's family wine production worked much better than the electrical treatment.

My uncle turned on the radio and I heard talk of something terrible. I understood, finally. Millions of people were killed in concentration camps for being Jews, gypsies, homosexuals, the disabled. Who had committed this genocide? Yes, Germans. Yes, humans like me. A wave of shame overcame me. I cried, devastated.

Days later, German prisoners were marched down our street by British soldiers. They were mostly cursed by bystanders. Then a mature woman came up to one young prisoner and said in Neapolitan (I translate): "He too, is a mother's son."

Just a Quiet Saturday Night

Hayley Camacho

"Where's my top?" I asked lazily. A chill started to seep into me despite being under the covers.

Eddie fished around for it. "Here it is," he said and handed it to me. I pulled on the flannel shirt.

We resumed our cuddling, his right hand resting on my abdomen.

The sound of a distant dog barking drifted in through the window of our yellow bedroom.

"Hon, get the TV," I said to Eddie. He sprang out of bed and walked the few feet to the living room. The TV was positioned on the side of the room that featured a wallpapered tropical scene. After cleaning and painting our apartment before moving in, we were no longer offended by the mural. It helped to fill the nearly empty room.

We were blissful newlyweds, married a few short months. Our apartment building on Taylor Avenue, near the Bronx River Expressway, was in a row of dreary, prewar apartment buildings. The brick wall of the next building was our view from the living room. Our bedroom faced the rear of another building.

Eddie unplugged our little black and white set and wheeled the cart into our bedroom. He positioned it right in front of the bed of the tiny room. I loved looking at Eddie's tall, lanky frame. He turned on the set and got back into bed.

"Who's on *Saturday Night Live*?" I asked.

He leafed through the *TV Guide* on his nightstand. "It's James Brown," he answered.

"Oh great," I said, snuggling into him.

We watched the last fifteen minutes of news before the show started. A skit with Dana Carvey and host Jamie Lee Curtis opened the show. Then the familiar jazzy theme started and Don Pardo announced "It's Saturday Night Live with musical guest James Brown!" over a wailing clarinet.

It was Saturday, sweet Saturday. No work the next day to worry about. We could be lazy for another day.

Upstairs the new baby started to cry and I groaned. In the two months since moving into the building, I had passed our very pregnant upstairs neighbor in the entry hallway a few times. Our eyes would meet briefly but no greeting was exchanged. I felt badly about that.

In the past week, sleep had been difficult for the new mom and me: the baby woke us up at regular intervals. Eddie was undisturbed. He could sleep through anything.

I heard the woman get up out of bed above us and walk toward the kitchen, the baby wailing away. After a few minutes I heard her walk back and the baby stopped crying.

Eddie and I enjoyed watching the program for the next few minutes. Then the crying started up again. I swore to myself that it would be several years before I had to deal with crying babies.

In the midst of the crying, I heard an apartment door fly open in the hallway, followed by a man's voice. "Shut that damn baby up!"

My eyes opened wide and I looked at Eddie. I jumped out of bed and ran past our tropical beach to the front door and looked out of the peephole. Our retired neighbor from across the hall stormed down the stairs from the next floor. He slammed his door.

I scurried back to our room shocked at his outburst, yet laughing. More commotion soon ensued.

The superintendent came up from his basement apartment and began pounding on the man's door. He and his wife were Irish and had nine children.

Our neighbor across the hall refused to oblige. Again I ran to the front door. I had the impression the new mom had called the superintendent to complain about our neighbor's outburst. Eddie was uninterested. He just wanted to enjoy *Saturday Night Live*. He sat up in bed, arms folded behind his head.

"There's no need for that Frank," yelled the super. His wife and several of the children were behind him.

"What did Frank do?" asked one of the younger children.

"He said something bad about the baby," said another.

The super gave up and walked away. "What an asshole!" he shouted.

Frank's door swung open and he stepped out into the hallway. "Call the fucken cops, why don't you!" he said.

"Oh, what's the matter with you?" said the super's wife. "Are you sick or something? That's a new baby!"

"Call the fucken cops!" Frank said, and went back to his apartment slamming the door again.

I walked back into the bedroom appalled. "Oh my God! I can't believe that man! Who would do such a thing?"

"Frank would," said Eddie.

We watched the rest of *Saturday Night Live*. Parodying Fred Rogers from *Mister Roger's Neighborhood*, Eddie Murphy welcomed his neighbors to *Mister Robinson's Neighborhood*, an urban and grittier version of the beloved children's program.

"Today boys and girls, I made a new friend," he said in a syrupy tone, as he changed into canvas sneakers, the way the real Mister Rogers did. The audience laughed.

There was pounding on the door of the Robinson home. "Open up Robinson," yelled a man. "I know you've been with Juanita. I'm gonna kill you!"

Eddie Murphy's eyes and mouth opened wide in mock surprise. "Boys and girls, Mister Robinson is going for a little jog," he said, approaching a window and opening it to step out, while the pounding and yelling continued.

"We're living in his neighborhood," said Eddie dryly. I turned to look at him and laughed.

The Shooting

Dahlma Llanos-Figueroa

Today, a young man was shot outside my school. I did not witness the shooting nor did I hear the two rifle shots as they echoed from one building to the next all the way down the block. I didn't know the teenager personally. Still don't know his name. Don't even know if the kid went to our school or was just hanging out in the neighborhood. There have been so many rumors since.

But my eyes see him lying on the gray concrete, the redness of his life dripping onto the pavement and flowing into the crevices as cars zoom by, little more than casual interest or annoyed impatience beaming out from the round faces behind the steering wheels.

Throughout the day, many of my students wander in and out of my classroom in many levels of pretense. I too am going through my routine as though little has changed. Writing the aim of the lesson on the blackboard, I find chalk dust sliding down the surface and then hear the crack of the broken piece of chalk. How did that happen?

The kids burst in.

"Hey, man, they just blew that nig—" Curtis looks up at me, sees my stiffened back, and makes the adjustment, "that Ne-gro away."

"That's why I know I gotta carry my piece. That shit'll never happen to me. 'Cause you know I'm down. Nobody better mess with me!"

"Yeah, I get my boys to back me up," Willie jumps in.

"Your boys? You ain't got no boys. You just got some little chump-change little mutha—"

Laughter.

I try not to listen. Try to concentrate on taking attendance, checking the same row of Delaney cards over and over until I give up and try to stare them into silence. But I'm not the focus.

"You gotsta be connected, like me," Tyrone says, taking center stage.

"Yeah? Only thing you connected to is yo' mama's wallet," Willie chimes in.

"Ooh! That's a dis!" a chorus of voices says.

"You talking 'bout my mama? I kick yo'ass!"

"You and how many other skinny ass niggers from Simpson Street?" Willie gets personal.

"Wo!" A chorus. "You gonna take that Curtis?"

I hate the n-word but let it go for now. I turn off the banter of the boys in the front row for a moment, trying to clear my thoughts. Trying to focus on the ones in the back of the room, the ones who rush in and open their notebooks and grab their pens as though they could transfer their fear into the ballpoints and have it flow out onto the page.

The same kids who usually saunter in ten minutes late, can't wait to be ten minutes early today. They sit as far from the windows as possible and try to control their increasing nervousness, their mixture of fears and reps, dangling from their eyes like the eyes of lost children.

"They say his homeboys'll be out there at 3 o'clock, miss, so we gotsta go by the enda this period. We can't be doing no detention or no shit like...sorry...or nothing like that this afternoon. I don't want no trouble and 'sides, that wasn't none'a my bizness. Thems probly them DRs who's always hanging out there."

"Yo, yo, Curtis, theys plenty brothers out there, too. Don't be hanging this one on just us," José says, standing up for his compatriots, pants hanging dangerously low on his hips, lip poked out in annoyance.

I try to take control. What's wrong with me? This is going too far. I have to rein them in. Somebody is saying something, talking to me.

"Miss, maybe you could give us the homework aheada time sos we can book." Curtis wipes the sweat from his brow, trying not to let his nervousness show.

"Yeah, miss. I'll come and get my library book tomorrow 'cause I gotta get home and watch my baby brother," Jenny says.

"Brother? Since when you got a baby brother?" José says.

"She don't even have a daddy," Tyrone puts in.

Chorus. "Oh! Dis! You gonna let him dis you like that, Jenny?"

"Fuck you, David. All right?" Jenny says.

"When and where, baby? When and where?" Tyrone leers at the girl.

"Huh, you wish you was so lucky!" Jenny punctuates her response with the appropriate offending finger stuck in his face.

"Yo, yo! Sorry, miss. They ain't got no manners," says Curtis, the peacemaker. "I didn't say nothin'. Right? You saw me, I didn't say nothing, miss."

"Look at this shit!" Tyrone says, staring at Curtis.

Curtis, under his breath says, "Chill bro, the miss knows my momma and I got 'nough trouble at home with none o' your shit, too."

The bell rings and thirty-seven chairs are dragged away from the desks.

"Sorry, miss. We'll catch you tomorrow. We gotta book."

I'm left alone in my classroom, with my books and my Delaney cards and my helplessness. I drop my weight onto the battered chair, feeling old and out of touch with the world. The door opens and a backwards baseball cap pokes in, Curtis' sweaty face under it.

"Miss, don't mean no disrespect, but you better move it. I don't like seeing no nice lady get caught up in all o' this mess."

I looked at the distress peeking out from behind Curtis' eyes and the worry painted on his brow. And I fear for him.

"Curtis, you go home, now. You hear me?"

"—preciate it, miss. But I gotta hang with my boys. I owe them—and today I pay. They watch my back and I watch theirs."

He's about to take off.

"Curtis..."

"Yeah, miss?"

"Don't....maybe..."

"Ain't no maybes about it, miss." He's about to close the door.

"Curtis…"

"Yeah, miss?"

"You take care of yourself."

A shaky smile. "Yeah, miss."

The Next and Last Stop

Miguel Mateo

There I was driving on Interstate 86-W, as freely as the last leaf to fall off a tree. The road was mine. I felt the warm rumble of the eleven-year-old machine under me and thought that the driver's seat would become the bearer of my imprint, and that no one would feel as comfortable as me in it.

Flashbacks of the times I'd be on a road trip to schools such as Syracuse, Rochester, or Cortland played in my mind. If I was ready to come back home I'd have to wait until the driver was ready. If I wanted to continue enjoying the trip I'd have to leave the fun because the driver was ready to go. But they were washed away by the sparks of fireworks that I felt in that moment.

When I took a look at the speedometer I let out my greatest laugh of excitement ever…I was nearing 90 MPH. No other cars. No state troopers on watch. No care for the thirty-three hundred dollars I'd just spent. All that mattered was that it was mine.

There's Honda. There's Nissan. There's Acura. There is even BMW, but not really. Those are expensive! All of these options had me stumped. Which make would I choose? How much was I willing to spend? How do I even go about buying a new car?

Every time I sat at my computer desk in my living room (with baby angels from countless baby showers and champagne glasses from weddings, all with a layer of dust almost an inch thick) I lived a dream. On the 20-inch display in front of me were endless opportunities. Most importantly I saw the release from the walls that confined me to other people's time.

If I had any of these cars on the screen I will come and go as I please. I will not allow food inside. I surely would not allow cigarettes to be smoked. I'd keep it as clean as my bedroom, wiping down the entire dash at the sight of a speck of dust.

I knew I had to be realistic. I should ask those same drivers that won't let me drive their cars what I should look for. I should ask where the best place to look is. I should definitely ask about maintenance of a car. These conversations, and more, would be a habit for as long as needed. I mean come on, I finished one year of college!

I could manage one more without my own car.

The summer of 2008 was filled with reasons to find a car of my own. It would take forever to get to the 5 train that would get me close to home. I was on that train so much that the recording was stuck in my head…I even dreamt about it: *The next and last stop is, Eastchester-Dyre Avenue.*

The long street from the train station to Boston Road became a setting for hundreds of movie scenes that played in my mind. I must've walked over two-hundred seventy-three times on that block alone.

The seasons rolled by. My summer runs on Pelham Parkway transformed into a rushed pace to get from class to work on time; maneuvering through crowds of students on Binghamton's campus. I wore a hooded sweatshirt every day during the fall and kept gloves and a scarf handy during the winter. I avoided wearing my best sneakers on rainy days during the spring.

Once the summer of 2009 hit I was finally ready. I met up with my cousin and a friend of his at my cousin's house in Monticello. I walked around the car with my friend, Ariel, so he could school me as to what made the car a good deal. After the test drive I was sold. I didn't want to wait any longer, but had to get license plates and insurance.

A few weeks later I had it all: two metal plates in hand, a temporary insurance card in my pocket, and a new key on the ring spinning around my middle finger. As I drove my—yes, *my*—1998 Acura 2.3 CL to Binghamton on I81-W, I couldn't wait to get away from all of the upstate trees and show off my new wheels on the gritty streets of the Bronx.

I drove downstate the very next day. It was empowering to pay the toll, as a driver, crossing the George Washington Bridge. I felt like a part of driving culture as I followed the signs for I-95. I was proud to know I was cruising along the Cross Bronx Expressway towards New Haven.

Flashbacks of staring out the passenger window of a friend's car at Co-Op City, my old playground, raced through my mind. But this time, all I could stare at was the Baychester Avenue exit.

As soon as I found a parking spot I became very excited. My attitude slowly changed as I shifted between D and R multiple times trying to accommodate my two-door in a large enough space. There was no way I could ever forget breaking a sweat during this first attempt at parallel parking.

Italian, Irish, French Canadian and German

Siri Edna Nelson

I'd never been to Arthur Avenue. My mom told me I should take a cab there. She insisted that it was a bad idea to walk. But Googlemaps told me it was only fifteen minutes away. Besides, I'm way too cheap to take a cab.

It was great to finally go on a date in the Bronx. Guys usually invite me to meet them somewhere in Manhattan, which means I take the subway an hour each way just to meet someone I don't even know—but hey—at least there's usually a free meal involved, right?

I met most guys on OkCupid and it was kind of weird, you know? These guys, they're, well, they all love texting and sending messages back and forth too much. I only have a few criteria. He's got to meet me, preferably nearby, take me to dinner, and I would really like it if he were black or Latino.

My goal was to meet guys locally. I've already got a white Swedish guy in my pocket and I don't need to go halfway around the world just to find another Aryan dude. Unfortunately, dating websites don't really have these requirements in their filters, so I have to go at it kind of blindly.

The guy I was about to meet had a profile full of praise for the Bronx, he definitely knew the borough. He was funny, too. His first message read: "Hey Sexy ;)" which tickled me because it was so cheesy.

Another plus was that he was eager to meet. The only problem was that he was white, or rather in his words "Italian, Irish, French Canadian and German." Regardless of that, he had that urban look and his profile pic showed him wearing a Yankee's fitted and a cute smirk, so I was curious.

He wanted to meet on a night when I had nothing else to do, so I thought—*what the hell, why not?* I had spent the day writing and relaxing at home. Somehow, I had the impression that I had all the time in the world, but by the time I was dressed, my date was supposed to have already started.

You can't blame me completely though: this guy had been texting me all night changing our plans. First we were supposed to meet at one time, and then another. He wanted me to meet him next to his church, and then outside on the corner. I had to Yelp the area just to figure out where to meet him because he couldn't make up his mind.

If only I'd known Arthur Avenue was a food oasis!

It would have saved me lots of time…

By the time I was finally ready to walk out the door, I tried to call a cab and failed, so I figured I might as well walk. Briskly traversing the area, I stayed alert just in case one of those new green Borough Taxis drove by. It was no use though, since not a single one would stop for me.

While passing the Burlington Coat Factory, TJ Maxx and White Castle on the way, the development of the neighborhood was like a serenade, it was becoming so familiar to me, and I enjoyed it. Enchanted, I was happy to be on my way to meet someone who also loved the Bronx.

I caught up with him at the liquor store, and we ducked into an Italian restaurant next door. It was one of the most beautiful places I had ever been to. There was a polished wood bar, brass outfitting, leather stools, a painted ceiling, and a handsome bartender. We easily settled into the place, ordered drinks, and started talking.

Unsurprisingly, my date was shorter than his profile pic implied, and he spent most of our conversation dissecting his brother's relationship.

Revealing a total lack of knowledge on the topic of marriage, he naively asked me—"What legal documents?"—when I brought up the fact that marriage and divorce weren't so easy after all.

He even told me about the crush he once had on the Bronx News 12 weather woman (who looked nothing like me, by the way).

Within an hour he finished his glass of wine, looked at me and said, "Well, I just got a bottle and I'm gonna go home and drink it... Wanna come?"

He lived in City Island, so I declined. There was no way I was going to go way out there. I love the Bronx and everything but the whole point was to avoid an hour-long commute. We said goodbye and I walked into the bright and bustling night street with a sense of satisfaction. At least now I knew about Arthur Avenue.

Back In the Day

Andrea Purchas

I was born in the Bronx. When I was one my family moved to Queens. It was the 70s and school was never much of a thought for me back then. Watching my mom cook in the kitchen helped us form a unique and special bond. Then I had to leave the comfort zone of my home to enter into this whole new world called school. That was not an easy adjustment.

My first day of school.

I remember the sweetest teacher one could ever want—her name was Mrs. Hunt. I cried so much in the beginning and remember Mrs. Hunt saying to my mom, "She didn't cry too much today." It took time (her poor ears) but eventually I stopped. My kindergarten experience was frightening.

The main focus in school for me was making friends. I wasn't approached like I thought I would've been. It felt like no one really cared and that was just the beginning of it. All I really wanted was to be liked by my classmates—it was that simple. The whole schoolwork thing was secondary for me.

Early on I experienced how mean my classmates could be, which soon became a constant reminder of school life. As I approached my upper grades I realized that I was not the fighting type, but did develop a sassy mouth. To be manipulated to fight when you weren't a fighter was pressuring. Unbelievable pressure.

My mom used to say, "You have to hit them back!" Easy for her to say, since she wasn't there. I needed someone to step in so it would stop. Wishful thinking. Life seemed so unfair.

At the end of each school day I looked forward to going home. I lived one block away from my school, so when I turned the corner daily, headed toward my house, there was my safe haven.

I drew comfort from the friends on my block. They were a replacement for my school peers without even knowing it. We enjoyed playing all sorts of games after school and on the weekends. I had a little too much fun, out of all of us. As report card time came around, my grades reflected that.

Sorry, mom.

Did I forget to mention that I had a fourth grade teacher who gave me a hard time, too? She was so mean. I felt like she picked on me and this other student on purpose. All the time! When I wasn't prepared with an assignment for her class I would find a way to be sick that day, dreading having to face her unprepared.

As time went on things did start to come around for me in unexpected ways. I was so surprised and happy when one of my essays was placed in the Principal's Showcase (for everyone to see with my picture). Wow!

To receive that kind of attention from the principal of all people! Then there was the spelling bee. I made the mistake of misspelling "beginning" with one 'n' instead of two. I just knew I was going on to the district level. Darn it. I was so disappointed with myself.

I remembered the day when I asked my mom for Billy Joel's "I Love You Just the Way You Are". I kept asking until she finally got it for me, along with another 45-inch vinyl (called 45s) of a "counting chickens" song.

I loved the words: "Don't go changing to try and please me...I love you just the way you are." I loved those words, such a beautiful song. I believe my mom has that record stored away in her current home, to this day.

Graduation Day, Class of 1980. I listened as all the smart kids got their honor and merit awards. If only that was me, I thought to myself. Then to my surprise I heard my name called, to come up and receive an award.

I thought there must've been a mistake, or better yet, maybe I was next in line if (for whatever reason) or there was a no-show. I hesitated to get up at first. You could hear a pin drop it was so quiet. The only sound you could hear came from my brand new wooden-healed clog shoes on the shiny floor. I went with my head down, hoping I didn't trip.

In that moment, when all eyes were on me, I felt as if my heart was going to stop. I entered the stage to receive the Citizenship Award for the entire graduating class. The sound from the applause that filled the room meant a lot to me. I was too shy to express my emotions at first, but I knew my mom was there sharing the proud moment with me. It took some time for the initial shock to wear off, as I began to realize what had just happened.

A full circle moment came just then. I was recognized after all by important people. A decision had to be made. Someone thought highly of me in order for me to receive this. So who had the last laugh now? That would be me. That's right, me! I still have this award and I proudly display it to this day.

When I got older I had another full circle moment when I volunteered at the same school. The current principal was that mean fourth-grade teacher I wanted to avoid at all costs. We spoke briefly, and when she smiled, it made that uncomfortable time with her okay.

What I learned is that her style of teaching was her way of expecting more out of me. Her approach was different and I was now able to respect it. Looking back, I would not have traded it for anything in the world. I later returned to where it had all started.

My hometown of the Bronx.

Bronx Redux

Gerault Rotondo

In 1969 I moved from East Harlem to an apartment on Sheridan Avenue in the Bronx. My wife was pregnant and we were seeking a better place to live. The street was one block off the Grand Concourse. It was an immense step up. Moving to the Bronx from Harlem was part of the natural process of upward mobility.

The Grand Concourse was certainly grand. It was a wide thoroughfare modeled after the Champs-Élysées in Paris. The buildings were architecturally elegant and modern, the style being Art Deco. It was a neighborhood in transition.

When you passed the parks or went shopping you would see the primarily elderly Jewish population that remained. The influx of younger Puerto Rican and black newcomers was evident on the streets and in the buildings. My neighbors were essentially working-class Puerto Ricans.

Next door to us were Frank and Millie. They had two children, Janet and Junior, and Millie's mother, Doña Gena, lived with them. Frank was a fireman whose heroics he understated.

Other young couples we knew were Manny and Iris, Danny and Susan, Freddy and Sylvia. They were traditional marriages at the time, in that the men worked, and the woman stayed at home. Manny managed The Luxor Movie Theater around the corner and Danny worked in heating and air-conditioning. Freddy worked in a lawyer's office.

I had been a student at City College, but with a child on the way, I needed full-time employment. I was hired as a Community Organizer by the Simpson Street Development Association (SISDA). Located at 163rd Street between Tiffany and Fox Streets, the agency's purpose was to manage abandoned properties or turn them into coops.

The director of the agency was Maria Estella, for whom housing in the South Bronx was named. The President of the Board of Directors was Father Louis Gigante. Father Gigante, although Italian, was a champion for Puerto

Rican empowerment. He headed SEBCO, which was building low-income housing in the South Bronx

I was teamed up with Jacinto Carbona, to go into various buildings we were trying to save. Jacinto was a huge man, black as night, Puerto Rican, a tough and loyal companion. We were all trying to stop a process, a force that seemed unstoppable.

Everything was being swept away by this whirlwind of destruction. Burned down, abandoned, lots strewn with litter. It began in the South Bronx, but eventually spread through much of the borough. The Bronx had the reputation of being one vast wasteland

I saw the corrosion, erosion, on my own block. It was gradual, but progressive. City services diminished, the building wasn't well maintained, working people moved out. Those who could afford it moved to Co-op City or other locales. Gangs resurfaced—Ghetto Brothers, Savage Skulls, and others.

I remember the culminating experience for me in August, 1974. There was a street fight with one participant, a gang member. He lost and his parting words were: "I'm gonna burn your building down."

That night, while Nixon resigned on TV, I sat on my second-floor fire escape, keeping watch, lest they throw a Molotov cocktail through my window.

I packed up and fled. First to Riverdale, later to Westchester. I lived in New Rochelle and White Plains, but nostalgia for the Bronx always lived in my heart.

On my trips back I noticed all the renovation, rebuilding, renewal. Houses where there had been vacant lots, new and modern apartment buildings. Like the Phoenix that rose from the ashes, the Bronx had risen.

As always, the Bronx has sights and sounds unique unto itself: The Bronx Zoo, The Botanical Garden, Van Cortlandt Park and Mansion, Poe Cottage and Park, Pelham Bay Park, Orchard Beach. Plus the neighborhoods: Arthur Avenue, Pelham, Riverdale, and so forth.

I've been back for two years and I'm happy to be home.

New Miracles on 34th Street

Phyllis Bowdwin

One evening, while waiting for the uptown D train at the Thirty-fourth Street Sixth Avenue station, a young man in his early 20s sat next to me reading a book. He put it away and pulled out another one. He glanced through it, closed it, and pulled out a third book!

A Queens-bound F train pulled into the station. He ran for it and disappeared inside one of the cars. He forgot his small shopping bag of books under the bench. I put the bag next to me, believing he would miss it by the next stop and come back. I waited thirty minutes. Three downtown F trains stopped with no sign of him.

The bag contained four hardcover and two paperback books on Jung, Plato, cultures, DNA, yoga, economics. The title *Backstabbing for Beginners* intrigued me. I glanced through it and was hooked.

The author had become a whistleblower when billions of dollars disappeared from the UN's Oil for Food Program. I wanted to keep the book, but thought of the poor guy who was probably a student, who would face a replacement cost of between $250-$300.

A potential hardship.

I lugged the shopping bag upstairs and tried to hand it to an MTA porter.

"I can't take that."

"Why not?"

"You have to turn that in to the Lost and Found office on 34th and Eighth Avenue."

"You mean I'd have to leave this station, walk over two long blocks to Eighth Avenue, pay another fare to get into that station?"

"Yep, but you'll have to do it tomorrow, because they're closed now."

"There must be another way."

"You could give it to the clerk in the booth."

So I tried.

"I can't accept this," the clerk said. "We can't open the door for anyone, and they won't fit into the money opening. And even if they could, we only keep them for a week. If no one claims them, we throw them out."

So I carried the bag home to the Bronx, reading *Backstabbing for Beginners* all the way. I went online but found no venue for a finder to file a report.

The next day after going up and down two sets of stairs, I located the Lost and Found office in the center of the station at 34th Street and 8th Avenue.

It was closed! The sign said they closed at 3 p.m. on Tuesdays and were open from 11 a.m. to 6:30 p.m. Wednesdays and Thursdays. I dragged the books home again, savoring *Backstabbing for Beginners*, and felt tempted to just keep the whole lot. But I visualized that probable student facing the extra expenses.

I returned on Wednesday, opened the steel door, and stepped into the cubbyhole of a room with a computer for filing lost item claims. A narrow barred Plexiglas window, situated above a 14"x14" safe-like steel box, allowed the clerk to safely pass and receive small items.

I turned in the books and was given a receipt and a number to call, to learn if the owner had filed a claim. I called by phone, but it just rang continuously. I dropped by a few days before the deadline. The owner hadn't filed a claim thus far, and I had a nine-day window of opportunity after the deadline to claim the books.

When I returned to claim my books, I found a young woman wandering around the labyrinth of a station looking for the Lost and Found. She followed me to the cubbyhole filled with a line of people filing claims on the computer. The girl lost her cell phone three months ago. They promised to look, but didn't hold out much hope.

A man sitting on the wooden bench said, "Girl, why did you wait so long to file?" She shrugged, sadly.

I gave the clerk my receipt and my ID and joined him on the bench. "They called me and said someone found my wallet and I got myself down here. I'm just waiting," he said.

"I lost my cell phone," another woman said, face drawn, jaws tight.

Another man filed for his lost bike and wallet.

"A bike and a wallet?" said the first man. "How'd you get separated from your bike? Don't expect to get any money back. Just your ID if you're lucky. That's all I want, my ID."

"If ya' do good, ya' get good," the second man said, smiling.

"What does that mean?"

"What goes around comes around?" I asked.

The second man nodded. "An' ya' must live right to get right. If you want to prosper, always spend some, save some, and give some away!"

"Johnson!" the clerk called out.

"Right here!" the first man yelled, stepping up to the window.

"Sign here," he said, passing him a form, "And let's see some ID."

He signed and showed his ID. The clerk put a black wallet in his hand with several bills fanning out of the top. The room got quiet.

"Money?" I asked

"Yeah, money," he said in wonderment, as he counted it.

"How much?" I asked.

"Seventy-five dollars!"

"Ya' must give 10% away," the second man advised.

"Could you lend me seven dollars?" I asked.

"You need some money?" Johnson asked, opening his wallet.

"Only kidding!" I said, grinning.

The steel door opened and another clerk came out with a bike and wallet! "Henri?"

"Right here!" the second man said, reaching for his bike and billfold.

"I don't believe this!" the woman said, hands up to her head, grimace lines erased.

The young girl's eyes brightened.

"Believe it," the second man said, smiling.

"How much?"

"My same $50.00!"

"Bowdwin!" a third clerk called out, holding a familiar shopping bag. "Here!" I said, rushing over to the door to claim my books.

Everyone smiled, as did all three clerks. The hope, energy, and good will in that room could have warmed a home in the worst blizzard. There were new miracles on 34th Street!

A Library as Beautiful as the Bronx

Jean Harripersaud

I remember it vividly. It was the morning of January 17, 2006. I was on my way to work, when an MTA bus zoomed past me. It was then that I noticed it, on the side of the bus, a poster-size picture of the building with the caption "A library as beautiful as the Bronx."

I looked in astonishment, then with pride and joy, as I recognized the building—it was where I was headed!

Such was the start of the day which heralded the grand opening of the Bronx Library Center and NYC's first municipal green building. At the end of the day, 6,000 people would have passed through its doors for the very first time, as a city, a borough, and a community welcomed and celebrated its new central library building.

A few months later, the US Green Building Council would present the Bronx Library Center with the LEED Silver Award—making it the first municipal building in New York City to qualify for and obtain such an award.

I delighted in seeing the look of amazement on the faces of library visitors each time I let them know that the Bronx Library Center is NYC's first municipal green building.

The Bronx Library Center is not only a leader in energy efficiency and sustainable design—it is a 21st-century library in every way. As libraries are constantly evolving to meet the ever growing and changing needs of society—the Bronx Library Center is reflective of this change.

It is currently the only New York Public Library location to comprehensively offer all of the following services and programs under one roof:

On our fifth floor is the Career and Education Information Service, which is managed by a Career Coach. The department offers computers for job searching, resume creation, editing, and posting. Over two-thousand training videos from Lynda.com can also be accessed on these computers.

Individuals by appointment can have one-on-one job and educational counseling sessions with the Career Coach to get advice on their job search and entry into institutions of higher learning.

On Tuesdays and Thursdays from 9 a.m. to 5 p.m., members of the public can have a one-on-one consultation with a Benefits Counselor from Single Stop where they can determine if they qualify for any of the forty government benefits, and get assistance signing up for same. These run the gamut from unemployment insurance to SNAPS.

On the fourth floor is The Reference Department which has a Reference Collection in both English and Spanish and an extensive electronic database collection which can be accessed on the forty-eight desktop computers available there for public use.

If you prefer to sit by the window, check out a laptop at the Circulation Desk...

This floor also features a special rare Puerto Rican/Latino Heritage Collection in Spanish housed in a smaller room adorned with the artistry of Puerto Rican Heritage. In addition, there are smaller collections on Bronx History and Edgar Allan Poe's works, the great American writer whose cottage is just yards away from the Bronx Library Center.

There is also a circulating Spanish collection on the Latino experience, from which library users can borrow materials to take home. Tables and chairs for the serious scholars and lounge seating for the casual reader or those who just want to relax in a social space are available.

On our third floor is the Adult Department, an extensive circulating collection in English running the full Dewey spectrum from computers, management, exam prep to cooking and travel books.

For those who are most interested in the joy of reading, there is General Fiction, Mystery, Sci-Fi, Romance, Classics, and for those who prefer to have the book read to them, check out an audio book and plop it into your CD player and shut out the world.

If you are a digital reader, save the $10 for lunch and use your library card to download an e-book for free on your tablet or smartphone. Need help downloading? Ask a librarian for instructions.

This floor has six computers and study tables and lounge seating for adults. It is a quieter atmosphere where adults can have their own space. There are designated quiet zones for those who prefer the sound of silence. Daily newspapers and lots of popular magazines, as well as some scholarly journals, are available for in-library reading.

For those who prefer to read in their native language there are smaller collections of books in the following languages: Bengali, Chinese, French, Russian and Vietnamese. If you prefer to have the sky as your canopy as you relax or study or chat with a friend—use the outdoor reading terrace which is open on fine weather days.

The second floor is devoted to Children's Programs and Services. Books, DVDs and other materials for children are available. The floor has a special area where parents with their toddlers can use age-appropriate computers or crawl on the colorful rugs flanked by shelves of picture and board books.

The older children have their section with computers and non-fiction and fiction chapter books. A story hour room equipped to offer a variety of children's programming including a puppet theatre offers daily programming for kids.

The first floor has the Popular Adult Library, plus new bestsellers, music CD collections, movie and documentary DVDs, Large Print and Urban Fiction collections. It also has the Teen Center, where teenagers can be teenagers in their own space as they use designated computers and enjoy collections of books, DVDs and music CDs.

Various teen programs are held each week.

In addition, the Circulation Department is located on this level, where you can get a library card, return or check out materials. This floor also sports a snazzy self-check machine and convenient book drops should you want to avoid waiting on line. This floor is more of a social space and it is okay to chat with friends without the fear of disturbing anyone.

The Concourse Level features a 150-seat auditorium that offers performances every Saturday at 2:30 p.m. In addition, lectures, film and community forums are frequently held, as well as instructional workshops. A computer lab provides over thirty each month.

The Adult Learning Center, also located on this floor, offers a valuable Adult Literacy Program, where adults learn to read and write, as well as attend ten English as a Second Language classes each week during the winter, spring, summer and fall sessions.

A permanent artwork, "The DNA Representation of the Portrait of a Young Reader" by Inigo Manglano-Ovallo adorns one wall on this floor, while the gallery space highlights rotating exhibits by educational and cultural institutions, as well as local artists.

Library-sponsored resource fairs are frequently held in this space.

The operating hours of 9 a.m. to 9 p.m. on Mondays through Saturdays, and Sundays from noon to 6 p.m., all year round, are very convenient for students and workers on all shifts.

I recently attended a Pew Research Center presentation on libraries and found that the public want their libraries to offer the following: information resources, book borrowing, free access to computers and the internet, quiet study spaces, programs for children and teens, research and job and career resources, free events and public meeting spaces.

After studying the chart, I thought to myself—by Jove, the Bronx Library Center has it covered!

HAPPINESS in the House ON 161th Street   By Cynthia Timms

I RECALL NOT SO LONG AGO I didn't Know Why I WAS Still ALiVE

The only thing that thrived inside me, WAS A Feeling oF DESpair aND miSERY

My beloved Aunt hAD PASSEO AWAy Not so long bEFoRE aND I WoNdEREd What I was living FoR?

JM
REST IN PEACE

then one day I got A CALL FRom A Place I didn't EXPEct at all

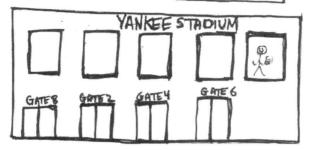

YANKEE STADIUM

GATE 8   GATE 2   GATE 4   GATE 6

HE Introduced himself AND how pleasant he appeared to me!!!

AS I listened carefully

THAN A surge of JOY WENT THRU me WHEN the Yankees said they wanted me!!!

OFF to the ballpark I now RUN, my new Life has begun!!!

Meeting FANS From NEAR AND FAR I HAVE Found MY Place Among the STARS!

AT EACH GAME I look AROUND AND FEEL THE LOVE I HAVE FOUND

AND NOW WHEN I LAY ME DOWN TO SLEEP I DREAM ABOUT THE HAPPINESS IN the House ON 161th Street

Educational Journey

José Cenac

On May 5, 2004, I restarted my college education at Essex County College, Newark, NJ. I graduated with an Associate's in Science on June 3, 2007. On January 2008, I moved back to the Bronx. On January, 2009 I registered at Lehman College for one class: Philosophy of Religion.

My experience at Lehman had been very pleasant and exciting until an encounter with one of my professors during the fall 2010 semester. I took the initiative to register for the whole semester at the Academic Center for Excellence (ACE) for tutoring in writing, exclusively to work on assignments for the ESC 409 course.

My first session at the ACE was on October 5, 2010 at 9:00 a.m. On the same day, at 6:30 p.m., the ESC 409 class was dismissed, except for five Latino students—Dominicans to be specific—who were not doing well on their journal entries. I was the last one in the room with the professor and her assistant principal.

I asked her for my previous journals to learn from her corrections, comments, and feedback.

"I do not have them. I suggest that you drop the class because you are not doing well in this course. You are not writing at college level," she said.

I showed her proof of my attendance to my first tutoring session but she did not take a minute to look at it. "I am determined to improve. We are only three weeks into the semester. Don't you believe in me?"

"I only suggested that you should drop the class."

"I am not dropping the class, and I am going to pass this course."

"Then prove me wrong."

"Whether you believe in me or not, I know one thing, I believe in myself. I have the potential to meet your standards and I will pass this course. Your negative approach toward my efforts and performance in class makes me confirm what you had said earlier that night while we were discussing Howard Gardner's *Multiple Intelligences*: 'I am not a people person'."

I was expecting her to say something like: "José, I see your effort, I see your active participation in class. I see that you have been proactive and took action to register at the ACE Center for tutoring in writing. I noticed that your writing is not meeting my standards, but the semester just started. Work hard, and continue attending the tutoring session every week. I am sure that you will be up to par, and if you need me I am here for you. I believe in you."

This brief, powerful, compassionate, empathetic and supportive statement would have made a huge difference. I felt that I was treated with disrespect, lack of consideration, lack of compassion and empathy. She was trying to kill my hope.

Three weeks later I produced an "A" paper. I was waiting for that paper week after week to see the grade, like a child waiting impatiently to open his Christmas presents. I knew I could produce an "A" paper. The professor ended up giving me an "F" grade for the course.

I appealed and the Appeal Committee changed the grade to a "C" without providing me with a breakdown on how they arrived at that final grade. I knew that it was a political and diplomatic grade, meaning, we give him a "C" and he doesn't have to retake the course. The professor doesn't look so bad, as if we give him what he deserves, at least a "B+".

My educational experience reminds me of Richard Rodríguez, when he said in his autobiography *Hunger of Memory*, "The belief, the calming assurance that I belonged in public, had at last taken hold." That "belonging in public" is the ability to communicate in English properly and comfortably.

All the courses that I have taken so far in my college experience have been in English except for the courses in my Spanish major. No professor has told me before that I was not writing at college level.

I had two experiences, completely different, with two different professors in the fall semester 2010. The first was with the professor described above and another from Burundi, Africa. She was empathetic, interpersonal, compassionate and jovial. She also had a complete understanding of the different backgrounds of her students.

In the future, I will emulate her approach with my students. I will always remember these two professors, by distinguishing who did not have an ounce of interpersonal skills and who was the most empathetic professor I had ever had.

I will continue to improve the skills and knowledge in my field, and as Maya Angelou invites us to do, "I will pursue the things I love doing, and I will do them so well that people can't take their eyes off me. All other tangible rewards will come as a result."

I will make sure to be remembered as the most empathetic teacher my students ever had.

In May 2012, I graduated Summa Cum Laude with a BA in Spanish and a minor in Education. Two years later, in May 2014, I graduated again Summa Cum Laude with an MA in Spanish.

On May 22, 2014, seven days before my graduation, I saw my professor from Burundi. She made me cry every time I saw her. I was the only student able to pronounce her complete name soon after she introduced herself to the class.

She opened her eyes wide, filled with energy and life, in complete surprise when she heard my voice, with a Hispanic accent, pronouncing her full name flawlessly: Inmaculée Harushimana.

We came to the United States from Third World countries: Burundi and the Dominican Republic.

Two tropical countries located on different continents. One root: Mother Africa, "the cradle of humanity" spread out all over the surface of the Earth. We are stardust. We are part of all that exists in the Universe. We are all interconnected.

I Remember When I Lost You!

Deborah Williams-Camps

Unlike my lack of memory concerning your birth (as you were born on my first birthday), I do remember when I lost you. You'd been sick for some time. I called our grandmother, Ma Dear, on a sunny day in September, and she told me you'd passed away!

My life would never be the same…

You put up a good fight. At twenty-seven years old, you, my first birthday present, were gone. As hard as it was for me, the grief was even more immeasurable for our parents and Ma Dear. I remember you packed a kaleidoscope-filled lifetime into your living.

I remember the day in the schoolyard—you sought me out—the school bully kept shooting you with his water gun. He lived in the same building as we did. My solution was to tell the nearest adult, resulting in the water gun being taken away from the him, followed by a threat to me to replace it or else. Dad took care of the situation from there. Needless to say, neither of us was ever bothered again by the bully.

I remember when the tables turned. You'd grown much taller than I, and you became my protector against the inappropriate shopkeeper (once I pointed him out to you). I was dismissed, never to find out what occurred between the two of you.

I remember your uni-cycling from Manhattan to the Bronx, past Yankee Stadium, over the Macomb's Dam Bridge. Eventually, you went on to motorcycles. You took life by the horns and lived it out to its fullest.

I remember your being reprimanded for taking apart and putting together again the bicycle of a neighborhood child. I remember the first time I met your precious baby girl, having to tell her at the age of seven that you were gone.

I remember you were an avid photographer, developing your own pictures. I remember how you, sis, Dad, and I walked to Bronx Terminal Market each year to get the perfect Christmas tree—"The stalk has to be straight," Dad reminded us each year.

I remember you being a bank teller, and working alongside our uncle at Time Warner. I remember you lived one adventure after the other—you knew no fear. You were a great baby brother and I often imagine how you would be today had you lived. I remember my most precious gift…you.

The Day I Play Hookie from Kindergarten

Christina Marie Castro

We are late, as usual. I move my short, skinny, bare, tanned legs as fast as I can below my school uniform. The wide front panel of the burgundy plaid jumper lifts up with each big step I take, as I seem to fly up Boynton Avenue, pulled by the arm by my twenty-four-year-old mother, Hilda. She hacks and coughs morning phlegm onto the concrete sidewalk, grossing me out.

I hate when she does that.

We turn the corner onto East 172nd Street. I look down at my new yellow short-sleeved shirt. It has the rounded collar style I like. I remember picking it out on our last shopping trip to Cookies Children's Department Store, just down the block from where we live, on Westchester Avenue.

Cookies is where my mother buys pretty much all my clothes. I admire my shoes. I like my whole outfit. I'm late, but well put together—my mother is the best at that.

The June sun is already high and beating caliente over the Bronx. My mother escorts me to school wearing small pink rollers in her hair, a loose cotton tank in pale pink, tight khaki shorts, and white slip-on sneakers. Like mother like daughter, we both rub the backs of our hands across our wet foreheads and wipe away the droplets of perspiration forming behind our ears. I feel a bead of sweat form down the middle of my back, fall onto the curve of my waist, then soak into my panty line.

Finally, we arrive at the blue stone steps of the public school where I attend kindergarten. We step into the cool marble foyer. My mother gives the top of my head a kiss, tells me to be careful, like always, and leaves in a hurry to get ready for work. I missed breakfast but can join the children watching cartoon classics like Betty Boop, Popeye, and Bugs Bunny.

I enter the sundrenched auditorium and step through rainbow-colored sunrays to a seat at the back of the room, near the door. I watch film after film on the wide projector screen and fall into a trance. Out of the corner of my eye I see a familiar figure enter the room. My mother is back and she still has not changed into her work clothes.

She waves at me. Fear comes over my little body in a flash. Something bad must have happened. My mom says two words—"We're leaving"—so I put my backpack on and follow her out.

I ask her, "What happened?"

She shushes me and says, "I'll tell you when we get home."

I decide someone must have died. My knobby knees start to quiver. This will be my first death in the family. Oh no. Who died? Great Grandma Fela in her rocking chair? Great Grandpa Candido in his hospital bed? I'm scared. And there I'd been, just seconds ago, falling off into a cartoon dream. I'm certain that what's waiting for me at home is a nightmare.

We turn the corner onto Boynton Avenue. My mother is walking just as fast as she does when she's rushing to get me to school. I beg her to tell me what's happened, but she won't. We climb the stairs of our red brick, two-family home. I count. My mother and I live upstairs with Fela, Candido, Titi Yvette, and Peter. Madrina Maggie and Padrino Louis live downstairs. Louis' mother Lean lives in the basement. Any one of them could be dead. As my mother turns her key and the front door swings open, I ready my heart to break.

The first thing I hear is quiet. Then I hear tiny footsteps descending the stairs. My cousin Jazzy, a dark caramel-skinned cherub with thick wavy dark hair cut into a messy bob appears at the bottom of the stairs wearing a blue ruffled bathing suit. She and I are only one month apart in age.

Jazzy lifts a yellow pail and red shovel up in the air and says, "Hurry up. We're going to Orchard Beach!"

I'm confused. "What?"

"Surprise, we're going to Orchard Beach!" my mother says.

I feel relief, but just to be sure, I pause before asking, "So, nobody died?"

"No," my mother says, "Nobody died. Get your bathing suit on 'cause we're going to have some fun!"

My mother just took me out of school so we can go to the beach in the middle of the week, and everyone's alive. I have a brand new sand pail and shovel and I'm supposed to get my bathing suit on right this second.

Madrina Maggie is cooking a huge pot of arroz con pollo. Padrino Luis is packing the cooler with ice, fruit juice boxes, cans of Pepsi, and bottles of beer. Titi Yvette is loading beach bags with blankets, towels, napkins, cups, plates, and forks.

Grandma Hilda and Grandpa Ruben arrive to pick up half of our Gonzalez crew in their big brown station wagon. All the kids sit in the back with Grandpa Ruben's big grey boom-box tuned to La Mega 97.9, playing salsa y merengue the whole drive up to Orchard Beach. I live it up, forget about dying, and play hookie from kindergarten, family approved.

A Conversation with My Son

Ann Sealy

SON

Hi, Ma.

MA

Hi, son. What's up? I love to use that phrase. I'm trying to speak your second language. It's called slang, right? I'm getting it. The first time you came home after you moved was Christmas and I was lying on the bed trying not to let the family know that I missed you. You stuck your head in the door and said, "Hi, Ma." You had a blue bandanna on your head and diamond stud in your ear. You stretched your long self across the bottom edge of the bed.

SON

I was waiting for the mother questions. How are you? Do you have a new girlfriend?

MA

There's none today. My question is what was the hardest for you when you left home?

SON

The hardest for me was telling my boys that I gotta' go, that I can't hang. Some would say 'Oh, you too big for us now'. No I gotta go. I had practice and classes. They came around later.

MA

Grandfather said that you were very focused. He noticed that when your older brothers did puzzles you would solve them later and never said a word. Seven years of age is a big difference and when they started working, I learned that they would give you money on the side.

SON

You didn't see everything, Ma.

MA

I tried. I loved being a mother. My ambition, five children through the school system, drug free and on time, and on to college. The high school dropout rate was fifty percent, but not in our home. Thank you, Heavenly Father. You all went straight through. The drug thing was because of your father, Sidney.

SON

I heard. Dad allegedly put the word out. 'If you offer my kids drugs, I will kill you.' That did it. No drugs.

MA

Grandma, told me you gave her your cell phone number in case she wanted to reach you. She asked me what a cell phone was. She is 83 years old, you know.

SON

Grandma sends me a full freshly-cooked Thanksgiving dinner by FedEx every year, no matter where I am. It is a really special treat. Is that all, Ma?

MA

All of your friends, schoolmates, and even teachers miss you. And the collective family in 2000 where you grew up, they do too.

SON

Ma, Ma....

MA

Just two more things before you go. Sam told us that you could get seats to anything, anywhere in the country. Even in Utah. Who do you know in Utah? It's largely a Mormon state. You were raised to respect everybody's religion. But they do not believe that God favors black people. That's not really all that shocking when the constitution of the United States counted us as three-fifths of a man. Yes, their belief was changed when Donnie and Marie Osmond were popular. Still, old beliefs die hard.

SON

Remember you hung Desiderata in our room and told us to learn from it. In part it says, 'As far as possible without surrender, be on good terms with all persons.'

MA

All of you beat the world for quoting me. That's how I ended up in China with your sister Raqiba when she was nine years old. I said no way is she going to China. Your oldest brother Sidney chimed in, 'You said try to go and experience as much you can.' So I went with her. The teachers in her elementary school, P.S. 110, had a raffle to help us go and friends helped. It was an eye-opening trip. We crossed the date line. That was spectacular.

Son, did you like your memorial service? A Minneapolis reporter wrote that a few hundred people came to the wake. The actual number was two-thousand. Now I know why you never read your press. The undertaker counted and remarked that we shook hands with all of them. Your brothers Dess, Amir…all of you had major friend bases since you were very young. Yes, I did call them 'posses'.

Mr. and Mrs. Werdann came. I understand that she looked near collapse. They were so thoughtful. It is a long way from where they live to Harlem. Your wife Lisa was in total control. The morning funeral was a wonder. Gorgeous day. On Memorial Day weekend. Every seat in Riverside Church was filled as far as we could see and the streets outside were respectfully lined. I learned that you and your friends usually hosted a major gathering in Cancun, Mexico on that weekend. The entire Timberwolves organization flew in to New York.

When asked where the celebrities should sit Lisa said, 'Save seats for the Timberwolves team, they are coming a long way.'

I am told some of the Pacers chartered a plane and came from Indiana. Mark Jackson, Reggie Miller, you know the crew. Many of the players brought their own limos. I always laugh at that because most people think that you players are showing off. Some, maybe. But a six-foot-eight black guy who is not as recognizable as Shaquille cannot hail a cab in New York. He usually can't drive a Range Rover or a BMW, either. He may be a drug dealer. Gotta' check. Pull over. Oh, sorry. Very sad, but still true.

SON
Maaa…

MA
Okay, New York's basketball elite was present. Former Falcons, The St. Nicholas of Tolentine family, Kenny Anderson, The Riverside Crew, The St. Johns people led by Coach Careneseca. Several NBA moms came in to comfort us. Many players attended. The ceremony was special. People from three different religions spoke. Lauren Hill and Desiree Jackson both sang beautifully. The music producers from Minneapolis Jimmy Jam and Terry Lewis provided music. The presiding minister of Riverside, Reverend James Forbes is the person who used to deliver my grandmother's newspapers in Raleigh, North Carolina. As a child, I had a crush on him. I didn't recognize him or his name.

SON
Ma, I gotta go.

MA
(*She rushes on*) One of your friends from Queens made a video of your life. That was so sweet of him. I have to get his name. We showed it during the funeral but we couldn't find the picture of you and the LA Clippers meeting President Clinton on behalf of Los Angeles, to include in the video. My Bronx boy. So many people, so much grandeur. Riverside Church is a cathedral. People came to honor you, us, in a really generous way. All I could think about was how I woke up every morning and realized, yet again, that there would be no more 'Hi Mas' from my baby boy. That the sun would shine but bleakness would cover me. I held the tears in…

We had a police escort from 122nd Street in Harlem to Ferncliff Cemetery in Hartsdale, NY. As we went along the parkway and Major Deegan Highway on a holiday weekend the police and state troopers stopped entrance traffic until the entire cortege passed. Some say it was because of the work you were always available to do with children whenever you could. I knew you supported the PAL near our home on Webster Avenue, and a women's shelter in Los Angeles. You never talked about it. I knew about the visits to I.S. 166 Roberto Clemente, your old school whenever you could to encourage the kids. I loved that.

We had two family cars. The bill from New York State said that 64 or 46 cars passed. I forget. Kevin Garnett asked permission and threw his jersey into the grave. Friends gently covered your final resting place. Your father helped. Lucille O'Neal and her sister stood close to me, in case I collapsed. I didn't. I was transfixed by the collective sorrow on so many faces, all sizes, shapes, colors, and stations in life.

All of them working to be as cool as we are known to be. All of us suffering in different ways.

SON
Ma, I really gotta go now. Love you.

MA
Okay, Malik. I love you too, son. See you when I see you.

How I Got Started in Show Business…

Kenny Williams

Kenny & Warren: The First and Only Lip-Sync Comedy Team In The History of Show Business…

There we were waiting for our names to be called. We were offstage at the world famous Apollo Theater. We were the Cha Cha Ladds—Kenny Williams (that's me!), and Warren Reid, my partner.

It was March of 1960 and the show was called *The African Holiday Show*. It starred Olatunji and his drums of passion, Art Blakey, and Esther Rolle. Alvin Ailey was our stage manager. What a terrific show that was! But we were ahead of our time and black people were not conscious about being "black", and after a few months the show went bankrupt for lack of support.

I started to tell you how we got to appear at the Apollo. You see, we were appearing at the Baby Grand, a famous Harlem nightclub on West 125th Street. Nipsey Russell was the star comedian there. He was there for many years and he made the club very famous.

We worked at the Baby Grand in December of 1959. There was a singer on our show and she was managed by Leonard Reed. Mr. Reed was the stage manager of the Apollo at that time. He was a famous comedian in his own right and had a brilliant comedic mind. He taught Joe Louis comedy when he retired from the ring. They had an act called Louis and Reid.

Not only could Leonard Reid outperform any white comedian at that time, he was also a brilliant worker. He had a problem, though. He was light-skinned, you see, so he looked white and sounded black. Nobody would hire him.

He happened into the Baby Grand one night to check out his singer and saw us on stage. He liked us right away and introduced himself to us after our performance. He told us he was going to book us at the Apollo.

You see, our act was different. We were basically a dance team: we did precision dancing to mambo and Cha Cha music. In addition to dancing, we did what was called a record act. Today they call it lip-syncing. You remember Milli Vanilli? They made it famous, or should I say, infamous.

Back in the day white comedians performed with records. That was called a record act. Record acts were popular in the Catskills. One of the well-known comedians that got his start doing this type of act was Jerry Lewis.

Black people were not familiar with record acts, consequently, we were a novelty, and the people loved our interpretation of the record act or lip-syncing as it is called today.

We didn't know anything about a record act until we performed at an Air Force talent show in San Antonio, Texas. On the show with us were two white boys and they did an act to a record by Stan Freeberg, which was a takeoff on "Day-O", which Harry Belafonte made popular. The act was really funny, we had seen nothing like it. So we decided to buy the record and do it ourselves, in addition to our dance routines.

After appearing at the Baby Grand on the first night, the owner approached us and told us that we should do more of the record act. He said that "your people love it".

So the next day I went downtown and bought a Stan Freeberg album and we performed three numbers from it. We also performed a tune by Señor Wences called "Easy for Me and Difficult for You". Señor Wences was a ventriloquist who appeared frequently on the *Ed Sullivan Show*. We didn't know what we were doing, so we played the records and tried to follow along. The people loved it and we had them falling in the aisles.

It was this performance that Leonard Reed attended. That was how we made it to the Apollo. The emcee announced: "And now ladies and gentleman, here are the Cha Cha Lads!"

We were extra nervous because we couldn't see and had to perform a verbal skit that Leonard Reid wrote for us. This was our first time doing a comedy skit. We were apprehensive when Mr. Reed approached us with this idea. He said we could do it, not to worry about it.

So we did it in addition to our dancing and our lip-syncing. We were a big hit. I remember thinking to myself, *wow, I'm going to be a big star!* I could see it all. I was going to make big money. My mother was also in the audience with some of my friends and they were calling out my name: "Kenny, Kenny!" I felt great. All this went to my head and I would later learn the tough realities of show business. I'll get to that later.

What was so amazing about me performing at the Apollo was that I was a very shy kid. Everyone knew this and were amazed to see me on the stage of the Apollo. It was unbelievable. How did I achieve this? Well, it was my love for the mambo that did it for me.

The mambo is a dance that is performed to Afro-Cuban music. Today the mambo is called salsa.

You see, I love the mambo. It's the happiness that the music imbues in me. When I hear the rhythms, the drums, the horns and the vocalist all in unison— having what sounds like such a wonderful time—it just takes me to another level of experience. Wow, this music is the ultimate joy!

You see, I was very lonely as a child. I was eleven years old and was kept in the house most of the time. I would look out of the window and see my friends playing and wished that I could be with them.

I was raised by my grandmother, who was a strict taskmaster. She was from St. Kitts in the West Indies, and she was from the old school and didn't take any nonsense. She kept me in the house most of the time, she didn't want me getting into any trouble.

My grandmother was tough. One time when I was around ten years old I climbed the fence in front of my house. The super's wife came out and told me to go across the street and climb the fence there if I wanted to climb.

Well, I went upstairs and told my grandmother. Why did I ever do that? We lived on the top floor, five stories up, but my grandmother flew down the stairs. She was a small woman, maybe 5'5". West Indians are known for butting with their heads when they fight.

My grandmother knocked on the super's door and his wife stepped out and my grandmother let her have it. She butted that woman so hard, that the woman fell on the ground. I shouted "Ma, you killed her!"

"Shut up boy!" my grandmother said. And to the super's wife she said, "And don't mess with my grandson no more!" That was some experience. Everyone on the block was afraid of my grandmother and they called her a crazy West Indian. They would tease me about being West Indian and this bothered me.

Yes, I was not only lonesome but troubled. And to add to my feeling of inadequacy, I was eleven years old when I was traumatized by a white cop, something that followed me into my adult life. I could see why blacks hated the police: they brutalized even little children because they were black.

Anyway, my love of the mambo saved me. I would come home from school and the first thing I would do was turn on the radio. I would listen to WWRL and Dr. Jive. That was a black station, and in those days, during the 1940s, black radio not only played R&B music but also Latin and calypso music.

I remember seeing older people dancing the mambo at school dances and I would go home and practice it. I was too shy to dance in public. In those days, most black people danced the mambo, not just Puerto Ricans.

I remember the first mambo I ever heard. It was by a Calypsonian named the Duke of Iron, and the tune was called "Mambo Calypso". It was very popular. I liked it because he described how you were supposed to dance it.

This is my story and legacy and I'm still dancing the mambo!

Adventures in Motherhood – 1977

Awilda Aponte

Friday afternoon.

A couple of us started talking about the 2004 blackout. As I was about to add my two cents, one of my friends commented that it was nothing unless you lived through the 1977 blackout.

"That's right!" I said.

I've lived through two New York City blackouts among other events. That same night, as I envied my son's gentle sleep, I worried about our New York City life. And in the darkness I saw my seven-year-old-self lying in the middle of the floor with a big brown pillow, watching commercials and drinking Hawaiian Punch with a crazy straw in a pink plastic cup.

I smiled, asked her if she liked growing up in New York City.

Yes…sí.

I know that we come in different shapes, colors and speak many different languages—even twins are different, but we all love our teacher.

I know that a boy is very different from a girl. And that some girls like to play with blocks and some boys like to play in the kitchen, which was against the rules, but the pretty teacher let them get away with it.

I know how to sign my name and how to tell time.

I know how to line up straight and wait and when to raise my hand.

I know that I couldn't talk in the classroom unless I raised my hand, only to ask a question or to answer one.

I know if I raised my hand a lot that the teacher would not call on me. Instead, she would call on those who didn't raise their hands. Sometimes I was glad because I didn't know the answer.

I know that anything that was repeated twice from the teacher was important to remember.

I learned that George Washington was so good (even when he knew he was going to get in trouble for chopping down a cherry tree), he didn't lie. I learned that Abraham Lincoln was a very good and peaceful man and was shot. I learned that Martin Luther King Jr was a very good and peaceful man and was also shot. I learned that Kennedy was a good president and was assassinated. His brother, too.

I know that to pass to the next grade you had to pass the state test. And I learned that the state tests had nothing to do with what the teacher taught that whole year.

I know the full names of all my friends, and all the hand-slapping games and riddles and jokes. I learned how to count backwards by counting down for the bell to ring so we could go home.

I learned to pray that the teacher would forget to give us homework. And I learned to give the "evil eye" to that kid who would remind the teacher that we didn't get any homework.

I know that everybody and every living thing dies, like the class goldfish.

As It Was

Alice Myerson

I am expected to report for duty each day, promptly at 0700, in my crisp white dress, my smooth white support hose, my polished white shoes, and my stiff white cap, as if everything is exactly as it was.

But, the sirens are silent. The wards have been cleared of patients. The furniture has been removed, the paraphernalia of sickness dismantled and discarded, and the workers, at least most of them, dispersed somewhere throughout the vast network of the New York City Health and Hospitals Corporation.

It is June 16, 1976. I am standing at the entrance to Morrisania Hospital. The sun is beside me and the old public hospital, for all intents and purposes, is closed, quietly, without fanfare.

I take a deep breath and I taste the fires that burn nightly in this peculiar corner of the Southwest Bronx. Nothing will ever be again today as it was yesterday.

The sun follows me into the dark lobby. I see the outline of a mop and a bucket resting comfortably against a naked wall.

I rush through the shadows. Breathless, I put a cross through my seven and write my initials in neat, perfectly formed, lower-case letters—a.s.m. C'est moi. 0700.

"Good morning," I say.

There is one woman in the Nursing Office. She wears a navy blue suit and her hair is coiffed. She takes a file from a tall metal cabinet, shuffles through some papers and places them carefully in a cardboard crate that sits alone on a desk behind the counter where I sign my name.

She does not turn around.

If Miss Reynolds were with me, I think as I enter the elevator, she would have said, "Did I sleep with you last night?" and would have chuckled and we would have laughed and she would have talked about my shoes, and Clarence who was always coming but never came, and the black-eyed peas she ate for dinner the night before.

The elevator door opens on 'four'. I hear the soft banter of the others who, like me, still wait, a thinning coffee club of nurses, playing Hearts on the floor of the female ward.

I get off at 'five', my floor, my ward, Five South, Male Medicine, reputed to be the worst ward in a hospital reputed to be the butcher shop of the Bronx, destined for closure because, after so many years of service, it was obsolete.

Blind to the signals of change, we went on as if everything was as it had always been, until that day in May when we rolled our last patient past the rows of empty, freshly made beds, and he looked at me with uncomprehending eyes. So I took his hand and walked beside him, and I waited with him until they took him away to wherever it was that he was to go.

I sit down on a scrap of yesterday's newspaper on the floor of the huge empty ward. I light a cigarette. Smoke fills the air with its acrid odor and the odor mixes with the lingering aroma of fifty years of urine saturated sheets, and paraldehyde.

The air is stultifying. The windows are locked. Sweat gathers around my hairline, trickling down the nape of my neck. My uniform clings to me just as it did July 8, 1973, when I first planted my feet in the chaos of this room and discovered the taste of sweat.

I remember an enormous man, and he pushed an enormous mop across a floor steeped in excrement, and it seemed as if they moved together, the man and the mop, through a forest of metal poles with glass bottles that hung upside down, dripping water through plastic tubes into the thirsty veins of an amorphous mass of men...

And the men, in various states of dress and undress, of motion and un-motion, clenched their fists into stillness while their fingers trembled with pain, their wrists, wrapped in strips of white Kerlix gauze, shackled to the baseboards of thirty-six wooden hand-cranked beds.

Miss Reynolds watched me with narrowed eyes. She told me that I best buy me a new pair of shoes if I planned to nurse the miles of this floor....not those cheap ones like I was wearing....strong shoes....like hers, because "there ain't no rest for the weary here, and no chairs where to *set*."

I saw her look at the others and wink. "Give her six months," said one.

"Ain't gonna find no doctor down here," said another.

"Think we see her back *agin* tomorrow?" asked Miss Reynolds, catching my pale dilated eyes.

She taught me how to wash one-hundred days of homelessness off the skin of a naked man, and how to roll a clean white sheet under his great buttocks and tuck it in so tightly that a penny could dance on the mattress.

I have become Miss Myerson, Nurse Myerson, Nurse, *Norsa*...

"The following will please report to the Nursing Office: Miss Pérez, Miss Johnson, Miss Myerson."

Miss Myerson....I put out my cigarette in a plastic cup filled with yesterday's water.

The woman in the Nursing Office tells me where to sign my name, and that I must hurry because the bus is waiting, and that it will take me to 125 Worth Street, headquarters of the Health and Hospitals Corporation.

That I am to go to the 7th floor, where I am to give them these papers, and be reassigned to wherever it is that I am to go next. That I should be grateful because I still have a job.

To Whom It May Concern:

Effective June 16, 1976, Miss Alice Myerson, L.P.N., is henceforth released from the employ of Morrisania Hospital...

Released, I think, as I step out of the old public hospital and into the thick haze of a Bronx morning. Strange words, those.

I am henceforth released.

Hunts Point Behind a Glass

Julio Edyson

The Bronx is different when you watch it from afar. Strange and beautiful at once. It's interesting: to be there and not be there, at the same time.

Some nights I sat by the window for a few minutes. Other nights, a few hours. It was one of the few things that escaped my mother's surveillance, and believe me, there was practically nothing she trusted I do on my own.

"Sit there until tomorrow si tú quieres," she used to say, "and maybe you'll learn something."

That's all she ever cared about—me learning.

One Monday night, mami and I argued back-and-forth. Her case was simple: "You have to go to bed Jonas, you have school tomorrow."

Mine was clever: "I'm not done learning."

This summer night was unusually quiet, and all the older kids had already exhausted themselves for the evening. They were done setting off car alarms with underthrown footballs; done tossing garbage around like fall leaves, and chalking bad words onto the concrete.

I didn't care, though.

My joy was in watching life as it happened: the stray cats pawing at knotted garbage bags; the winds bending thin trees back-and-forth; how sunset gave my neighborhood a different face. Mami leaned over at my side, and stared out onto the street, both palms pressed against the sill. Her body was plump, her hair short and confused.

There's no one out there, she said, turning her attention to me.

Yes there is, I answered, pointing towards a shaded corner near a fire hydrant.

She looked over and kept quiet. It was a silence not at all deliberate, and that's exactly what gave it its meaning. The lady stood motionless across the street from our two-story home, her exactness obscured by the darkness that fell over her.

"She's there every night, mami. Isn't it dangerous out here? Why doesn't she just go home?"

Quickly, my mother pulled the plastic blinds down over the window, and directed me to my room with a pointed finger. She's probably just smoking un cigarillo, she mumbled, her steps short and close behind mine. I walked into my small room, tucked on the right side of the narrow hallway. Mami stopped at the foot of the door, her finger soft over the light-switch.

"You're right, she's probably just smoking a cigarette," I said, nodding.

"I love you," she said, her head tilted over her shoulder. She hit the switch, and headed downstairs to her room.

She knew we would face this, eventually; she knew I would have these questions. My mother's prescience had failed her. It's interesting though, being old enough to recognize a lie, and still too young to find the truth.

But even as a ten-year-old I was persistent, sneaking to the window night after night. I watched. Sometimes the lady was still there. Sometimes she got into cars. If I stuck around for long enough, the cars dropped her back off. I wonder if her mother loved her when she was ten, as much as my mother loved me.

Writing 'Major Ascension Luna'

Jhon Sanchez

I am blind, not literally blind, but the kind of person that drifts until a tugboat suddenly brings me to the shore. In that same way, I started to write one of my recent short stories. "Major Ascension Luna" is a character in the story, a street vendor, who walks from Hunts Point, along Southern Boulevard to Simpson Street, looking to cure humanity of betrayal.

One day of midsummer last year, I was in a cuchifrito by Westchester and Simpson when an old Dominican woman wearing a manto over her shoulders said, "Nene, I want to read you the cards."

Augustiño, a friend, sat across from me, mixing oil and sugar over his beans to prevent what he called 'flatulencia,' an elegant word for farting.

My mouth was filled with the crunchy grease flavor of roasted pork, pernil, when she said, "You don't need to pay me. A beer would do."

She cleared my table and made me cut the deck, which I did with trembling hands, like I was about to commit a terrible mistake. The image of the upturned card revealed my fate to be tied to a knight on a horse.

I remember only this of her words, "A man, a mulatto man, with eyes like embers, will betray your trust."

For a flashing moment, I thought that this man could be my friend Augustiño; the sentence itself did not mean anything to me but the word 'betrayal' reverberated in my mind.

Precisely the same week, on my way back from the beach, I met a Mexican man with Indian features, who looking much younger than his fifties, gave me his business card.

"MAJOR ASCENSION LUNA."

His name surprised me, and he replied apologetically, "I was born the day of the ascension of the Virgin."

Later, I wrote in my notebook, "Major Ascension Luna was neither Major nor Luna."

On a visit to the Cloisters museum, I noticed a statute of the Virgin Mary holding a twig of a plant called Rue, the plant of grace and forgiveness. I remember how Colombians cleansed themselves in a mixture of alcohol and ruda, as it is called in Spanish.

The cleansing against the bad spirits, limpia in Mexican jargon, baño in Colombian, is followed by the prayers to the saints and the Virgin Mary.

"If one can get forgiveness with rue, why can't we prevent betrayal?" I wondered.

I knew then that Major Ascension would need to possess this plant for his battle.

I became fascinated by ruda, to the extent that I asked Augustiño to go along with me to Hunts Point to buy some. As we walked through, a man on a corner cried out, "Ahí vienen," and women, children and men ran to hide their vendor carts inside to avoid an inspector.

I imagined Major Ascension Luna in a weathered military uniform shouting to the vendors like the man on the corner.

After the inspectors went away and all the vendors reemerged, one Mexican woman said, "Thanks to the Virgin and to one who warns us, I never pay a ticket," and served us a soup with cream and corn, tesquequite, that would keep Augustiño on the toilet for five days.

There was nothing wrong with the soup but rather it was an issue with my friend's body, too sensitive, or in Augustiño own words, "My body is cleansing itself."

I enjoyed my soup and even ate more food at the cuchifrito where we asked a woman where the closest botánica was.

"Solern," she answered while stirring the lamb stew with a huge spoon. It took me a couple of minutes to process her pronunciation until Augustiño elbowed me saying, "Southern Boulevard."

The botánica, 7 Potencias, was quite a murky place. An announcement at the entrance stated: READING OF TAROT, PALMS AND LIMPIAS. There were statues of Saint Gregory Hernandez wearing his doctor uniform and Saint Francis of Assisi next to a statue of a black woman wearing a golden-yellow dress with two pumpkins at her feet.

I saw candles of many colors and lightly touched yellow ones that were in a box on the counter.

A Puerto Rican man whose neck had four chunky silver chains around it said with a smile, "Those are for Oshún. The protector of pregnant woman." He pointed to the statue of the black woman in yellow.

"Ruda?" I asked and the Dominican attendant gave me a small bottle with oil. I smelled it with curiosity before saying, "I actually want the real plant."

Without looking at me, she yelled to someone in the back. "Hey, mami pásame un cogoyo."

The twig had small leaves and yellow flowers that emanated an acrid-whiskey scent. She wrapped it in a piece of newspaper that had the image of Pope Francis on it, saying, "You can take a bath with it or take a tea but don't give it to a pregnant woman."

"So, if I am pregnant, I cannot take it," I confirmed, and Augustiño giggled.

"Caballero!" The woman took a breath before continuing, and I realized that this was the first time a Dominican person had called me gentleman instead of 'amiguito' or 'primo.'

Then she went on, articulating each syllable. "This is very serious. If a pregnant woman drinks this tea, she can have an abortion."

As we left in silence, I noticed how the attendant approached the statue of Oshún and touched its feet. "Major Ascension needs to be careful to not cause any abortions," I thought.

I did not perform a cleansing or drink a tea. I put the twig next to the parsley that grows under my kitchen window. One year passed by, and I could see the husk of what remained of the rue, the colors faded and similar to tree bark.

I still do not know if betrayal had visited my house. If so, I had learned that it is like any visitor that comes and goes and Major Ascension Luna, my character, is probably thinking just the same as he roams through Hunts Point during the full moon when forgiveness visits this Earth, at least for him.

I have not talked to Augustiño in a couple of months now, and I do not have a reason to think he is the mulatto man with red eyes like embers. The only mulatto man I see is myself, and my eyes turn red only when I cry.

"Well, Major Ascension Luna, be thankful for being betrayed because at least I can tell your story. Major, I cannot live without trusting. What else is fate but a mistake anyway?"

Morning and Evening

Laurie Humpel

I slipped out front for a quick smoke, and watched Bruce walk up 2nd Avenue. The grey tweed coat that he never buttoned billowed out behind him. Judging by his lilting gait he had already spent a few hours at the pub down the block. He swept past me with a kiss on the cheek but not a word.

He was a regular. Maker's Mark on the rocks and the occasional Beck's. I tried to stay away, but time and again I'd do the rounds in my section, then stop to visit him at the bar. I couldn't afford to linger, so after a wink or a joke I spun back around the dining room.

A disjointed and dizzying courtship.

Finally, after weeks of this, I let him take me out after I'd finished my shift. We paused at the door, but he couldn't wait for me to finish smoking. He grabbed the back of my neck and pulled my face to his, my cigarette—and everything else—forgotten.

I lost all sense of anything, the warmth of his lips, so that for a moment I couldn't breathe. That night we didn't even make it into the bar.

I knew he was a mistake; I would never know how much the bourbon fueled that smile. But God, could he look at me—brown eyes so deep and desperate they made me want to look away, that smile that said there would never be anyone else. Except that there were, and I knew it, even if I tried not to think about them.

He told me once, "If you're not here, I can't see you." But I already knew I walked out of his mind the moment I walked out the door. It's not as though he were my first.

No sense in mourning an impossible future. And there were nights, the Saturdays that started too early and only stopped when we closed at 2 a.m., or that late rush on Sundays that crashed the kitchen, when afterwards I'd limp across the street to grab a beer at one of his usual spots.

I'd much prefer the two-block walk to his place than taking the 4 train all the way up, to where red brick shadows and broken street lights hid the dog shit.

More than once he'd slide off his barstool and disappear, returning with a dozen roses.

No one ever bought me flowers. And besides, I knew he wouldn't raise a hand or his voice. Instead, he'd tell me he loved my body and make me blush when he'd whisper, "Such a beautiful woman…"

For once in my life, I believed it.

We spent nights at dingy karaoke joints, shouted earnest debates over the din of the Friday night crowd, laughed until my face ached. Since he was buying, I'd match his every bourbon with a whiskey of my own.

Our most intemperate evenings lurched groggily into the frantic sort of mornings that left no time for coffee. I'd read out his appointments while he searched for a shirt, and he'd hand me his cufflinks with shaking fingers. I snickered the first time I saw the elegant silver hardware.

"What the hell am I supposed to do?" he asked. "This shirt doesn't have buttons."

Other mornings, though, were bottle caps flicked into the fireplace and tepid beer spilled down our necks from sheer laziness. Those mornings dragged on half naked until early afternoon, until it was time for work or to hit the bar. On slow brunches I might get a long break on my double, and we'd get grape leaves and lamb kofta delivered. It beat eating huevos rancheros standing by the dish pit on aching feet.

He would stop to consider an interesting shadow, and point out the shape of our coats, dropped face-to-face on the floor.

Once, amidst the swarm of people on our early walk to the 6 train, he gestured up at the buildings and said, "I never look up enough."

There above us hung the unseen fleur-de-lis and disregarded lintels, all the intricate brickwork that went unnoticed. I never bothered to look up, either.

As the winter waned, he began to retreat from the ever-brighter mornings. In the sallow glow of a Guinness sign he could still feign laughter, but it took more and more to get him there. I encouraged him to paint again, my legs stretched across his lap as we ate pad Thai straight from the box. When he wasn't looking I studied the whites of his eyes.

He hadn't gone to work in days, hadn't even bothered to send an email. So that morning, when I wrapped him in my drowsy arms and legs I got a grimace, not a kiss, in return. He groaned and pulled away, tossed back and forth like the fitful sleep of nightmares.

"Oh God, oh God."

That morning was voiceless anguish and platitudes that withered unheard on my lips.

The screech of his buzzer startled us. He knew who it was—a woman from his office, worried he was dead. Someone buzzed her in eventually, and with every knock he clenched his jaw and clutched his chest. Fifteen minutes at least of that staccato beat on his door. He responded to my whispered pleas to answer it with a fearful shake of his head.

When the knocking stopped, and it didn't matter if the floorboards creaked, I left him lying there. I had to get ready for work, and I didn't know what else to say. I stripped off my clothes, put on one of his button-downs, and threw my things in his washer.

Maybe I should do his laundry. Maybe then he could get out of bed the next morning.

She came back. The thuds grew louder, more relentless, and I couldn't stand the muted dread that filled the pauses in between. Just as I got up to put another load in the washer the door burst open to strange voices. She'd called the cops, and the super had let them in. And there I stood, surrounded by laundry, braless and bare-assed in a half-buttoned shirt.

Swamp Guineas

Maria Meli

We were a large extended family: Italian Americans from Sicily that moved into a low-lying sparsely populated section of the Northeast Bronx in the 1920s. Many of our non-Italian neighbors, not understanding our way of life and traditions, often referred to us as "swamp Guineas". Today after creative, productive decades in the Bronx, we think back on that pejorative term with a feeling of great pride.

We began each day feeding chickens, ducks, pigeons, scattering grain, collecting eggs. Uncles and cousins raised pigeons (tiplets, homers, tumblers) and would race them.

Tumblers when let out, soared toward sky then tumbled down rolling toward Earth. Watching them, you thought they were out of control and would crash, but they would turn right-side up and fly skyward again.

For races the birds were put in crates driven south (Florida, Virginia, South Carolina) and let out to fly back home. We waited on the roof for them. All birds wore metal bands which identified them and their owners. When they flew back to their coops the band would be put in a special clock that recorded their arrival time.

The men would meet at pigeon clubs with their clocks, whosever bird came in first would win. Pigeon clubs affiliated with pet shops, two popular shops were located on Boston Road east of Eastchester Road, and on 183rd Street and Third Avenue.

Cooking in a wood-burning stove; wood had to be close by for Granma to cook with. We heated with coal. It was piled alongside the house and we had to shovel it into buckets and keep it full next to the stove. Feeding birds, setting up wood, and the coal had to be done before school.

After school we had to gather, chop or saw wood and pick rabbit food. We walked the woods gathering bushels of plantain and clover for them. In winter they ate pellets and veggies scraps. Male rabbits were removed from their coops when females gave birth because they would eat their young.

I don't remember feeding our goats anything special. Our pigs ate everything and loved mud. We raised animals to eat. When killing pigs, men had a little ritual. After they slit the throat they would punch it to drain the blood faster (and soften the meat). Then they'd drink the pig's blood. They did it with much ceremony. To honor the animal and give thanks.

The school we attended, P.S. 97 on Mace and Seymour Avenues, came on field trips to see our animals, and way of life.

We had no gas till I was 10; TV at 14, sewers came much later. Clothes were washed by hand, food refrigerated in iceboxes.

Kingsland Avenue was a road surrounded by woods that were abundant with fruit trees, wild berries, streams, and estuaries. For all seasons there were plenty of edible, pharmaceutical plants and wild game. From the estuaries we'd catch fish.

Three Italian families lived on Kingsland, all farmed empty lots around us. North of us were brick homes owned by Anglos who referred to us as swamp Guineas, dagos, and wops.

We lived in accordance with the seasons. Spring we turned soil, cleaned animal coops, turned manure into earth (best fertilizer), and planted seeds. Wild dandelion and burdock (known as cardoon) in the woods was a springtime treat. They were par boiled, fried like cutlets or simmered with garlic and oil. They were so bitter that they left a sweet aftertaste in your mouth.

In summer we gathered fruits of our labor, worked less, played more, did just about everything outdoors, good food to eat, family all around. Family visited from East New York, Harlem, Little Italy, Brooklyn, and Staten Island, and stayed awhile. We were the "country".

In autumn we picked mushrooms, had to break things down, bedding earth for winter, canning, cutting, chopping wood. It was a bit of frenzy at times. In winter women sewed and baked. Men made repairs. During the holidays everyone had chores, mostly for the preparation of foods. Coops were never cleaned in winter, manure provided insulation, heat for the animals.

Life was simple, we were all poor but rich with extended kinship and earth that nurtured us. A war was going on, we had ration stamps and air raids were scary. Sirens went off, couldn't show any light. My father was an air raid warden, had to go outside sometimes wearing a gas masks. Spotlights moved in the sky.

Perhaps they were looking for enemy planes.

Men worked as laborers, interstate truckers, for DOT, or were in the war. Women stayed home or worked in clothing factories (sweatshops) in downtown's garment district. The Bronx also had sweatshops on White Plains Road, Westchester, and Buhre Avenues. Education was not important to Italian immigrants. They worked, married, had children; to survive everyone had to work.

The industrial revolution of the fifties changed the Northeast Bronx forever. Yellow construction machines raped Mother Earth; corporate America built lookalike homes on Kingsland Avenue. Fruit that was a hand's reach from our mouths became buried under asphalt, concrete, no longer reaching or singing to the sun.

Fertile waters with crab, eel, clams, mussels and oysters are silent under Co-Op City and the Pelham Bay Dump. No one will ever hear music emanating from the Pelham Heath Inn Nightclub and Golf Course on Eastchester Road and Pelham Parkway. Bike or walk-on-the-paths that paralleled the Hutchinson River Parkway to Rye, New York. Or will they ever be able to pick fruit from pear and apple orchards that Jacobi, Einstein, and Montefiore Hospital are sitting on.

For me cohesiveness of family in community is gone. Third and fourth generations of Italians have relocated out of the cities and the state, but the memories of "la via vecchia", its beauty, bounty, and players, will spiral, undulate, in and around me, and continue to inform me, until I have no form.

The Product of a Social Experiment

Olga Kitt

I was born on a kitchen table at 1417 Wilkins Avenue in the Bronx in 1929. Mother had heard that hospital babies could be given to the wrong mothers and she wanted to make sure that she got me.

Upon seeing me, my brother who was just three-and-a-half at the time, couldn't understand why they made such a fuss. He had been removed from the apartment for the event. Later, he would needle me with the phrase, "I remember when your cord was tied."

He would always be older than me, bigger than me, and smarter than me. I was always a little bit behind.

I adored my brother, so did my mother and father. He was brilliant. He skipped classes at P.S. 54 and J.H.S. 40 and was sent to The City College prep school, Townsend Harris High School. He was so good that even the bright boys in his classes would ask him to help them with their homework.

Most of the time he thought I was a pest. I would follow behind him at a respectful distance of seven to twelve feet as he headed for the school playground.

He would turn around and say, "Go home."

His friends ignored me until I grew up.

As you may have already guessed I did not do as well in school. When it came time for me to select a high school the family came together to figure out what to do with me. We were living in Depression-era poverty. Although my parents would never apply for "home relief" we acknowledged our financial limitations.

An aunt told my mother that she should never have had me because "You can't afford her."

Moving to a better neighborhood was not an option.

"Maybe she could get into Music and Art," my brother said.

Mayor LaGuardia, a true progressive, was our hero. Besides smashing slot machines with a metal axe and getting rid of "tin horn gamblers" he set up a special high school for those who were talented in music or art.

Until then there were academic, general or commercial high schools for poor kids. In commercial high schools one could be trained to do specific jobs and learn the basics necessary for good citizens. Automotive trades and commercial art high schools were admired. But, classical music and fine art were usually taught by private tutors.

Those who studied the fine arts needed money to buy paintings or concert tickets. LaGuardia, however, didn't think it would be a waste of municipal funds to teach poor children the fine arts if they were talented. When he set up the High School of Music and Art it was considered a social experiment. I was game.

My brother found out from some of his friends in school that the biggest and hardest part of the entrance exam was contour drawing. Then he found out what contour drawing was. How hard could it be to draw the outline of an object? I had been struggling to figure out how to draw the human body in light and shadow. That took a lot of patience. Outlining figures should be a snap.

He took me to the Museum of Modern Art. I had never been there before. Paintings by Kandinsky and Cezanne inspired me. I ran from painting to painting as one after another captured my attention.

Cezanne left areas of his landscapes unpainted. The whites of the canvases were a brilliant counter to his warm colors. Years later I noticed the whites of those canvases had dulled and I was glad I saw them in my youth when they were   still   bright   and   my   eyesight   clear.

I felt confident as I took the entrance exam although as I looked about me I noticed other students' work didn't look anything like mine. I followed the examiner's directions and tried to apply the directions properly to my work.

Although I didn't know it at the time, they would look for work that showed a student's ability to learn. Years later the chairlady of the art department told me that I had received the top score on the test. When she retired from Music and Art she took the position of professor and administrator of the art education program next door at City College, where she hired me as her assistant.

My brother went on to become a doctor and set up a practice in Chicago. I wanted to be an artist. I took various teaching jobs, enjoyed them, and was able to support myself and my family for many years. My father said he never wanted me to be a waitress. It was not a good way to make a living. Teaching was better.

Childhood poverty leaves an everlasting mark. The belly might be full but a deep hollowness remains. One sympathizes with the beaten boxer who thinks he could have been a contender. Had I not had magnificent training as an artist, had I not been told that I was first among my peers, had I been given a simple basic education—what sort of life would I have led?

My brother owns the largest private collection of my paintings.

July 1977

Joseph Carrión

The summer months are hot in New York, and Popham Avenue was alive with the sights and sounds of the city: ice cream trucks, sirens, water pumps open full blast, and music from open windows. Our large apartment was on the sixth floor, and I liked looking out into the morning and onto the street from my mother's bedroom.

There always seemed to be people around, and by mid-morning, when the heat would begin in earnest, more people filled the street. By late afternoon, there was bound to be excitement in one form or another—summertime in New York City renews that promise daily.

But the oppressive heat can also bring unrest. One afternoon I heard a commotion and looked out of the window to see two girls fighting. They grappled with each other for dominance and swung around as if in a ritualistic dance.

Someone separated the fight and bought each an ice cream cone from the omnipresent Mr. Softee truck. It seemed as though vanilla cones with sprinkles had defused the confrontation, but as I watched, one girl calmly walked up to the other and smashed her ice cream into the other's face!

They instantly entangled themselves and became a jumble of arms, legs and hair as they rolled around on the pavement clawing at each other as onlookers urged them on into frenzy.

My brother Adam and I were placed in Featherbed Day Camp just off of University Heights, and I enjoyed the freedom of wearing loose shorts and chanclas every morning to go somewhere fun.

One day in July there was a blackout throughout the city. I was a well-behaved kid, but this event produced excitement and chaos, and I could not resist the thrill and anarchy of doing what everyone else was doing.

I followed some kids into a supermarket that had its windows busted out, and took what I thought of as an expensive item: a huge box of diapers! I cut the top of my foot on the shattered window glass.

I can still see the stigmata-like scar to this day. When I got home, I proudly offered the box of pampers to my mother who berated me, not for having participated in looting as an 8-year-old, but for not bringing home something more useful!

Time, space, and circumstance converge somewhere deep inside our minds to form the basis of lifelong memories, and summers are a fertile period for this embedding. I became excited whenever my father would tell Adam and I, "Go get your bicycles and put them in the station wagon."

If I asked where we were going, he would grumble, "When we get there you will know where I am taking you."

As soon as we arrived at Pelham Bay Park, I'd run up the oversized steps of the concrete stadium with its huge statue and look out over the top edge.

Later, Adam and I might ride our bikes onto the dirt trails near the waters of the sound. We'd have to ride quickly through the brushy trails or the mosquitoes would feast on us within seconds.

Sometimes, my father would bring along our uncle Quique, who brought along his gasoline-powered model airplane. Quique would prepare the fiberglass-covered plane methodically, and I marveled as the little plane lifted up into the air accompanied by buzzing and smoke.

He'd fly it until it ran out of gas and glided back to Earth far off near the tree line beyond the park's barbecue areas. As soon as Adam and I saw the plane descend, we'd run off across the grass to reach it, and I would always beat him.

By late afternoon, the beer cooler papi and tío Quique would bring along would be empty. My father spoke loudly on the way back home. If Adam began to complain of hunger, I elbowed him—I didn't want anything to make papi angry when he drank. Thinking back, I also didn't want anything to spoil the magic of the day.

When we got home, mami would make us macaroni and cheese while listening to disco music. My mother was younger than my father and inexperienced in many areas of motherhood: she wasn't a great cook, but it hardly mattered to us because she was easygoing and beautiful. She also was sensitive to the supernatural.

Anyone that dropped by our apartment would eventually hear about its being haunted with spirits. I listened to the stories even though they were scary, but I would forget them soon afterward.

One night I awoke to see two men placing a large trunk into the closet just outside my bedroom. The men were dressed strangely and wore vests and paperboy hats. I stared at them from my bed and was surprised when one looked up at me from his task.

He regarded me for a second and raised his finger to his lips as if to tell me to be quiet. I was not afraid and simply lay back down. When I awoke in the morning, I thought it must have been a dream. I'm still not sure.

The warm weather continued well into September of 1977, and it would still be warm when school began in the fall. I went to P.S. 143 where Ms. Cooper would give us pretzel sticks and Swedish fish when we did good work.

Ms. Cooper pronounced my name curiously: "Good work Jo-zev!" she'd say while handing me a treat. My first school fight happened there, too.

It was with a taller boy named Leonard. He shoved me in the play area and I stumbled—knocking down the books and crayons all over the floor. I got up and charged straight at him, only to be shoved back again, this time into the painting easels and Lego bricks.

My mother had me picked up from school that day by the comay's son. Leonard and I became friends after that. The next year we moved again: this time to Washington Heights.

Untitled

David Duenias

When he began banging on the drum in my first session I could feel the vibrations of sound bouncing off my body. Jacob works on the atomic level or what he calls the "cellular memory" of DNA.

"There is no such thing as forgiving. Maybe one forgets but rarely forgives," Jacob said to me when we first met.

He explained that in actual moments of trauma, a block occurs where the information of that particular incident that caused the trauma is stored on a primal level.

It is stored in the memory of each cell of our being. We carry that information for a long time, most of it from many past lives. In order to release the blockage, the work has to be directed to that particular level of cellular memory.

In other words, the healing process could not be approached from the mental apparatus—the brain. And if it does, it may take a long time to achieve this. With this work it happens instantly.

I tilted my head to the left and was asked to close my eyes and exhale through my mouth. Jacob held my left wrist, constricting and releasing the area where he felt a pulse while saying the words: hemoglobin, red cells, white cells, protein.

I felt squeamish at the beginning. I felt the lower area of my abdomen and navel contracting. A similar sensation when a muscle is becoming very tight. As we finished I opened my eyes.

Jacob asked me to get up from the stretcher bed, to step out of the room and walk a little. When I came back I sat down on the bed while he took out a magic eraser board—the same one children use.

"Have you ever thought of suicide?" he asked bluntly.

"Not really, Jacob."

I'd never had suicidal tendencies, but just like any other human my only thoughts of suicide were a direct outcome to some conjuring of the imagination dabbling with the curious scenario of what goes on in the mind of a person who was about to commit it.

I told Jacob that I was tired from this life. That everything was a struggle, from the simplest task to the largest. Nothing came easy, nothing flowed. I was only 34 years old, yet I behaved and acted like an old person sometimes.

"You had a very low level of hemoglobin, which is a rarity for such a young age. This causes suicidal tendencies."

He then drew a diagram on the magic eraser board.

He said that I had almost no level of hemoglobin! Therefore the body acted as if it had no oxygen. In turn it caused me to constantly feel tired, even as I began a task.

"I brought it back to a normal level," he said. "As I asked you to walk you were already looking much better. The way you carried yourself," he added.

On the second session Jacob said we were to work on the heart. To examine how it functions. He asked me to tilt my head to the side and breathe deeply while exhaling fully.

He went on to bang the drums heretically. At some point in the session I felt he was getting up to open the door. In my mind I imagined that all the spirits that needed to enter or leave the room did so. He pinched my neck while calling out "blood pressure".

He held two fingers out, creating pressing at the nave, protruding the fingers gently while drumming continuously. As he concluded the session he turned and asked, "If you are a photographer in New York, can you make enough income only from that?"

"I am not confident enough with it," I said. "Money flows abundantly. God created a natural flow of abundance for man. It is simple. We make it difficult. We falsely learn to believe that money cannot come easy and that is because of fear."

Then he added, "I see that in many past lives the recurrence of the same motif. Survival. You are a survivor, David. You have survived so much in the past. Let me ask you this: if we know that the body gets old and decays within time, while the soul never dies yet continues to evolve, what is there to fear?"

I didn't know how to react to this. This was a concept I had come across many times in my life, mainly through reading esoteric books. I also believed that this was true yet I still felt the fear in me. I was bewildered anew each time I believed 100% in what Jacob had said. I knew there was no other way.

I knew that the soul was permanent, that the fear of death was illusion. I knew that fear of any kind was the grandest illusion of life yet I just couldn't feel in my flesh and bones the feeling of security, confidence and trust.

"It is very simple, David. You can achieve anything you desire in a very simple manner and for that you have to understand something very important—the power of trust. Any word you say with full trust on yourself will bring forth immediate results. The key word here is 'trust'. Trust in yourself, trust in God. Fully! There is no such thing as right or wrong but only your word. When you trust it fully it shall never be wrong and that's how it shall be manifested."

He advised me to take boxing classes when I got back to New York. "It is a great way to practice the power of will," he said.

I further expressed to him that I had experienced for a long time the recurring feeling of yo-yo, where I am afraid to act at times for the fear of getting hurt, afraid of being rejected. I had experienced it many times and each was very painful.

"What is pain?" he then asked.

"One day I was traveling in the deepest southern regions of India. I was in a small town and noticed a large eagle in the middle of the road. Two Indian men caught it and tied a rope to its foot. They put it in a box. I told them to go find a larger box. A diversion to get them out of sight. I had some cookies in my backpack. I crumbled them and put them on the road. The eagle in the box did not move towards the cookies. The box was fully open yet it did not move. I kicked the box, and in that very action, the eagle spread his magnificent wings and flew away. The eagle had been caught up in its fear, thus paralyzed while all the time it had the ability and the freedom to fly away. I created a "shock" to get it out of its state of fear. Sometimes we need a shock to retrieve our natural state of being—freedom. It's our birthright."

"There is much work to be done," he added, while drawing a diagram.

Cowpath Lane

Steven L. Leslie

The weather forecast was for eight inches of snow and my task for the day as hospice chaplain was to visit three terminally-ill patients on the back roads of Delaware County in upstate New York.

In Maryland, where I grew up, February is the month when the first buds appear and the tulips begin to peak their heads out of the muddy ground.

A snowstorm of this magnitude would have closed schools and the major highways of Maryland, but here, in this rural area, we were expected to show up and also to be punctual.

Fortunately for me, the first two patients I was scheduled to see were near recently plowed highways, so I made it to them easily.

The third patient, however, lived off a dirt road—a road so insignificant it did not appear on the county map. By 2:00 p.m. the snow came down in earnest and when a sudden gust of wind came by it created a white-out condition.

I feared for my safety, driving blind with only a GPS to guide me. All I wanted was to go home and curl up in my bed, but the economy was in its deepest recession since the 1930s and I needed this job.

As I crept along toward my final patient's home, my trusty GPS called out the road names and estimated the distance remaining after each turn. Driving deeper into this deserted rural area, the road dwindled down from a two-lane marked highway to a one-lane paved road.

I cranked the wipers up high, praying all the while that I could keep the wheels on the road. If I had an accident there I might end up spending the night in the car. Finally, the GPS voice instructed me to "turn left on Cowpath Lane in 500 feet."

I breathed a sigh of relief that I'd finally made it to the last turn, but when I turned left onto that final stretch, I stopped my car in disbelief at what lay ahead.

Not only was the road unplowed, but the deep snow lay in pristine condition without even a tire track to mark the way. To make matters worse, this road, if you could call it that, climbed straight up a steep incline.

I leaned forward, wiping the condensation from the windshield, desperately straining to see the crest of the mountain before me…and then I heard the GPS lady's voice again. In a calm and neutral manner she instructed me to "continue on Cowpath Lane for eighteen miles".

Two years later, here I am living in the Bronx, the antithesis of that desolate rural area. Each afternoon I am greeted by the now familiar screech of metal on metal as the #1 train pulls into the 231st Street station.

As I wait for my honey, double-parked in my Subaru SUV, I listen to Latino rhythms, watch swarthy-skinned men gesturing in the barbershop, and catch the smell of burritos and enchiladas from the Mexican café.

Another train comes in and a large crowd of men in hoodies and women in colorful skintight pants disembarks. Alongside my car, two men unload fresh bananas, speaking rapidly in Spanish. I listen carefully, trying to catch where they are from.

Some Spanish accents sound neutral and clear to me, while others have a sing-song quality. And some sound staccato to my untrained ears.

The bus driver to my left leans on his horn, unable to get past the double-parked cars on each side of 231st Street. The traffic backs up. The M10 bus to Riverdale is stuck in the center of the intersection at Broadway and 231st.

A calamity of horns blares out.

In the center of the backup, I see a black, beat up, unmarked vehicle, the Bronx version of a taxi. The driver seems unfazed by the blaring horns and the cop on the street nearby, too weary to untangle the mess.

As my beloved and I drive up 231st Street, we turn left at Paul's Bagel Shop and cross an invisible boundary. Now the sidewalks are packed with young women in wigs, pushing double strollers and towing strings of children by the hand.

Male heads are covered by yarmulkes or black wide-brimmed hats, the garb of various Jewish sects. Nearly everyone is dressed in dark colors—a contrast to the colorful scene I'd just left. Mom's Bakery and the Jewish deli are closed, as it is near sunset and the beginning of Shabbat.

Just two blocks away is another invisible boundary, where on Sundays I hear the Gaelic brogue of my ancestors and listen to live session music while I sip Guinness. Here, the men and women talk about "America" as if it were a distant and foreign country.

After twelve years of wandering the Mid-Atlantic States, the Bronx is now home to me. My friends from Baltimore don't understand the attraction. I live surrounded by people from so many cultures, also encountering on a daily basis, gay and lesbian couples, artists, musicians, actors, and models.

I have discovered that New York is where I can be myself fully. My background as an energy healer, a yogi, a longtime meditator and a poet are valued here. I am not looked on as strange, weird or exotic.

Here, out of all the places I have lived, I have a voice. I have a place. I have a home.

Best Friend Lost

Bernice Cox

Spring, 1947. Morrisania.

I was eight years old. I had a playmate and we were the best of friends. We were the same age. Carolyn and I loved the same games: jumping rope, bouncing a ball to nursery rhymes, sharing secrets, hopscotch, statues and coloring books.

We did all the things that little girls do and baby dolls were our favorite. We got the giggles and laughed at the same silly jokes. If we had candy, we would save some for each other. Yes, we were the best of friends forever.

We attended Saint Augustine Church and School located on Franklin Avenue and 168th Street. The girls were taught by the Sisters of Charity, nuns in full habit.

The boys attended school across the street and were taught by the order of Franciscan Brothers. The school went from the first to the eighth grade; a small community of students in uniform.

One Sunday, a bright sunny day, Carolyn and I met on a seldom used staircase leading up to the church. That was our special place to play before the service began.

Carolyn said she had something to tell me. Oh boy, a secret! I thought.

"Cross my heart and hope to die!" (Meaning, I wouldn't tell anyone). I kissed my right hand up to God to seal the pledge. We stood face-to-face. At first, Carolyn didn't say anything.

I waited.

She took a big breath and looked at me—her brown eyes wider than mine and said: "We can't be friends anymore."

I was speechless. Then, I finally asked her: "Why?"

She hesitated. "My mother said I can't play with you anymore because you're black."

We just looked at each other.

I had never heard anything like that before and I was confused. I knew that we shared sadness that day. I never knew feelings like that existed because of skin color.

I remember her saying: "I know…I have an idea! I'm white on the outside and black on the inside and you're black on the outside and white on the inside."

We tried to make sense of it all. Why can't we play together and be friends like before? Carolyn had to do what her mother said and that was that.

We sat on the cold, stone steps in silence. I think a bit of our innocence was chipped away that day.

Carolyn said her parents were inside. She seemed uneasy. I watched her as she climbed the stairs and entered the church. I remained seated, all thoughts of play forgotten. Then, I silently followed.

Looking back, I don't think her mother knew that we ate lunch and played together, but not much. It was not quite the same anymore. I guess we were aware we were doing something we weren't supposed to do.

When Carolyn was with her family, we made eye contact, but didn't speak. We knew better. Over time, I saw Carolyn less and less until she moved away.

It's been sixty-six years and I sometimes wonder if Carolyn remembered me over the years as I've remembered her.

Did she adopt her mother's beliefs and pass them on to her children? Did she ever regret losing such a great friendship? I truly wonder.

Spring, 2010

I went back to Saint Augustine School and the church I attended so long ago. I was amazed by how much had changed, yet remained the same.

Memories came flooding back. It was recess time and children were playing. For a moment, time stood still. Suddenly, it was 1947 again and two innocent, little girls were laughing at play.

Best friends forever.

2000 - by Orlando Ferrand

PAGE 1

PAGE 2

THIS IS HOW I ENDED UP ON THE FIRST MORNING OF THE 21ST CENTURY. IN A K-HOLE, BROKE AND HOPELESS.

I MANAGED TO WALK OUT OF TWILO AND I DON'T KNOW HOW I GOT TO THE 14 ST & 7TH AVE. SUBWAY STATION. SO I HOPPED ON THE #2 GOING UPTOWN.

I WAS IN AND OUT OF BLACKOUTS. MY HEART WAS GOING TO EXPLODE. I COULDN'T BREATHE. EVERYBODY WAS LOOKING AT ME EXCEPT FOR THE JEW TALKING ON A PHONE

WITH NO SIGNAL. "THIS TRAIN IS GOING EXPRESS TO PELHAM PARKWAY" ANNOUNCED A VOICE IN INTERMITENT AND PIERCING SOUNDS" BEBEPPPSSZZZBOOO SORRY..."

PAGE 3

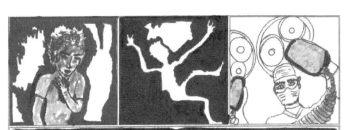

NYC, 2000— QUERIDO MUNDO:
THE CHEST PAIN WAS EXCRUCIATING;
MY ARMS AND LEGS WERE NUMB;
I FORGOT I WAS ON A TRAIN HEADING
TO THE BRONX. I WAS THE GUY ON
HANDSTAND IN THE DANCE FLOOR JUST
A FEW MINUTES AGO. I STARTED TO
FALL DEEPER INTO THE ABYSS. MY
LIFE IN THE 90s FADED AWAY IN
SNAPSHOTS. WHAT STARTED AS A
WEEKEND DIVERSION IN 1992 WITH
SONIQUE'S "IT FEELS GOOD" HAD TURNED
INTO AN UNSUSTAINABLE ROUTINE OF
HEAVY DRINKING AND ALL KINDS OF
DESIGNER DRUGS BY 1999, TINTED WITH
THE WORDS TO "WHO DO YOU LOVE" BY
DEBORAH COX. "WHO, WHAT & HOW DO
I REALLY LOVE?" "WHO LOVES ME THE
WAY I LOVE THEM?" I ASKED MYSELF
IN DESPERATION. I TRIED TO FIND ANSWERS
TIME AND AGAIN IN "WHAT IS LOVE." BY THE
TIME HADDAWAY'S SONG WAS OVER, SUFFERING

CREPT IN UNSEEN BUT TANGIBLE LIKE
AN ARMY OF BED BUGS. STRIKEN BY
TEMPORARY ILLUMINATION, I LEARNED
THE LYRICS TO "LOSING MY RELIGION".
REM, WAS THE CLOSEST I'VE GOTTEN
TO THE TRUTH SO FAR. AND TO THINK
THAT ALL I WANTED WAS TO BE PART
OF GLAMOUR, COLOR, EXCITEMENT; SOMETHING
LARGER THAN LIFE. I DISCOVERED THE
CLUB SCENE. I HAD BEEN IN NYC ALREADY
FOR A DECADE GRADUATING FROM COLUMBIA
AND CITY COLLEGE WITH HONORS. BUT
I WAS CHRONICALLY DESERTED. I LEFT
MY MOTHER, FATHER AND SIS BEHIND WITH
AN OCEAN BETWEEN US. I WAS A POLITICAL
REFUGEE FROM CUBA WITH NO INTEREST IN
AMERICAN POLITICS AND ITS INSURMOUNTABLE
SOCIAL INEQUALITIES. I THINK I DIED FOR
A FEW SECONDS BECAUSE I SAW THE BRIGHT
LIGHT AHEAD OF ME; I COULDN'T REACH IT.
I WAS SENT BACK TO JACOBI'S DETOX &
REHAB FOLLOWED. I STAYED IN MY SISTER'S
THE BRONX, WHERE I FOUND AN APT. AND
A JOB AS A LIFEGUARD RECONNECTING WITH
LIFE THE WAY I DID GROWING UP IN CUBA
FROM LEAVING MY FOOTPRINTS AT ORCHARD.

PAGE 4

After Thirteen Years!

Mandy Lopez

I was in the Dominican Republic on a nice hot dry night on August 2013. In the Santiago airport. I was coming out from getting my bags and I was nervous and happy and sad and excited, rushing all at the same time. It was there, right outside the closing doors of the airport, where I saw my father after thirteen years.

It was the most shocking experience for me. I had expectations for him that I didn't get great outcomes for. Everything felt weird. I wasn't happy, sad, or crying. I was shocked!

My dad had been a big healthy guy, fat, muscular, white and tall. His voice never changed over the phone so I thought neither would he, but it was different. He was skinny, really skinny, shorter than me, and had a non-familiar look on his face.

He wasn't the same and his voice didn't change. He told me "Hi, Chuli. It's me, your dad."

Chuli was a nickname he gave me when I was a little baby. I had no words. I was happy to see him, but not the way he was. I didn't fully accept the way he looked because he'd gotten like that because of drugs.

So I was mad. I thought about the whole situation, but figured I'd still give him a try because he was still my father. During my trip I tried to bond with him. We went out to the movies, went out to eat, saw family members—but that wasn't enough.

I felt that the long gap of time of not seeing him could've been a reason for me slowly readapting, and his physical changes made it harder for me to feel comfortable around him.

At the end of that trip I left in an understanding way, but not accepting. I tried to change things around, so I took a trip to the Dominican Republic again, in February 2014, with my best friend.

I saw my father again. I tried to hang out with him, but things were iffy. I wasn't comfortable around him when we went away for the weekend to see his side of the family.

I cried and felt unfamiliar and uncomfortable. With all the rumors and bad experiences (as a young girl) it made me appreciate my mother more and more and I understood why she did what she did.

Untitled

Erykah Solano

I was eight years old, in the third grade. One day, while I was cleaning the room, I discovered one of my older sister's discarded marble notebooks.

There was a folded section in the back that said "Top Secret". I didn't read it, but it gave me an idea. The next day I decided to write "Kiss my ass, Mrs. Martinez" in the back of my marble notebook.

That very day Mrs. Martinez collected our notebooks and I got caught. The school called my mother in to meet with the teacher.

Afterwards she wasn't mad but laughed hysterically. The woman still makes fun of me to this day. Funny thing is, Mrs. Martinez was one of my favorite teachers. I hope I didn't hurt her feelings!

Untitled

Brian Rodriguez

Spring, 2007.

All I remember was my mother coming to me bawling, trying to find the easiest way to explain what was happening.

My grandmother had just passed away from cervical cancer, and my mother was going to have to leave to take care of the funeral.

At that moment I had no idea how to react. I didn't know my lack of a reaction would come back to haunt me.

Later on, during that same year, I heard that my mother wasn't coming back, either. There must have been something in Puerto Rico that made her happier than she was in New York.

Subconsciously, it all took its toll. I went from a straight A student to a C-student. I went from being the life of the party to living like a recluse.

To this day it still bothers me. But God works in mysterious ways. Now, looking back, the events that took place are the reason no one can break me.

It has made me stronger than I was.

Bronx Story

Dolores Scarpato

I would like to share some of my memories of the beautiful Bronx...

I was born and grew up in my early years in the Arthur Avenue section. The area has now become a tourist attraction because of its great restaurants (Mario's, Half Moon, etc.), its amazing food market, Mount Carmel Church, the Bronx Zoo and the Botanical Garden.

When I was a kid, we would stop at Howard Johnson's across the street from the zoo and have the most delicious ice cream cone (in one of 28 flavors!).

My tenement window on Crescent Avenue overlooked the Cinelli Garden's flowers and flowing water fountain. Mr. Cinelli also owned the Cinelli Theatre (now the Fermi Library) which was one of the neighborhood hangouts.

Towering above all of it was St. Barnabas Hospital for the Incurables (I never liked that name), which is now St. Barnabas Medical Center.

In my early youth I attended P.S. 32. When I was eight we moved to a tenement on East 187th Street where I attended P.S. 85.

In that neighborhood you could get your whole education—elementary school, junior high school, Roosevelt High School, and on to Fordham University, if you were lucky.

I remember the field trips we used to take. One that stands out was our visit to the Indian Research Museum on Jarvis Avenue, which was closed to the public except by special arrangement.

My teenage years were hectic. I worked part-time at Manhattan's Lord and Taylor in a school program (one week work, one week school), and part-time (at night) at Woolworth's 5 & 10 on Fordham Road along with my best friend.

I was still able to go dancing on Friday nights at Poe Park after work and roller skating at the Jerome Avenue Rink on Saturdays.

After work we would stop at Brighton Cafeteria, next to Woolworth's, and sometimes see the last show at the RKO Theatre across the street (the ushers would let us in for free).

The Valentine movie theatre was across the street on one side of the RKO (and to this day I can't find anyone who remembers the small theatre on the other side of the RKO. (Maybe some reader will remember it and I can finally stop searching!)

There was also the beautiful Paradise Theatre on the Concourse with stars in the ceiling and goldfish ponds in the lobby (if a fella took you to this theatre you thought he had money). We also had the Metro on Webster Avenue.

And, on Kingsbridge, the Windsor, which sometimes had plays with Lucille Ball, Sylvia Sydney, and other movie stars.

In those years Fordham Road was the ultimate shopping area. You could get a beautiful pair of shoes from Mile's Shoe Store (for $5) and visit Alexander's and Roger's Department Stores, Cushman's Bakery, Krum's, Jahn's Ice Cream Parlor, Gorman's Hot Dogs, Kress 5 & 10 and, on the high-end, Plymouth Apparel.

We didn't have much money, so we did a lot of window shopping (there were no iron gates on the windows then).

Across from the Bronx Zoo was "old" Fordham Hospital which was torn down and replaced with Jacobi Hospital on Pelham Parkway.

Fordham University took up a big part of Fordham with my high school, Theodore Roosevelt, across the street.

Also, located on Pelham Parkway was a "cabaret"—Pelham Heath Inn—which was a nice place to bring a date. The Chateau Pelham, which was one of the first to cater weddings, was near Pelham Bay Station.

Remember Bronx Beach and Pool in Throggs Neck? A great place to spend a summer's day when you weren't visiting Orchard Beach and beautiful City Island. How about Freedomland? It tried to be a small Disneyland, but didn't last long and was replaced by Co-op City.

When I was eighteen I graduated from Roosevelt and continued working at Lord and Taylor full-time after that. This is where I met my husband.

We were married at Mount Carmel Church and had our reception at Mayers Parkway Restaurant on West 233rd Street, which is now a Montefiore (formerly Misericordia) parking facility.

We got an apartment on Adams Place across from where I was born and I was back in the Arthur Avenue area. When they tore down the Third Avenue El,

I had to leave Lord and Taylor and got a job at St. Barnabas as secretary to the medical director, and held various other positions over the course of 35 years.

I loved working there. The grounds were beautiful, with their promenade of trees, fountains and a gigantic gorgeous magnolia tree at the entrance.

Most of it is gone now, having made way for hospital advancement. We moved from Adams Place after five years, when my son was born, and bought a house in Country Club near Pelham Bay Park (where I still reside, after 52 years).

I am now seventy-eight years old and still love the Bronx. I was born and bred here, and have had most of the best experiences of my life here.

I know things have changed, but then, what hasn't? To me the Bronx will always be number one, and if this brief trip down Memory Lane brought back any memories for you, I'm glad.

Untitled

Anonymous

He often walked the sidewalks of the neighborhoods bordered by the Bruckner, East Tremont, White Plains Road, the Cross Bronx and Castle Hill, blazing new trails in his mind. He drowned out the traffic with music on his phone, strolling along the tough concrete littered with trash and dog shit, each square replaced by fresh blades of grass and a green carpet beneath his feet welcoming him home.

What is home?

They say home is where the heart is, but to him that was a lie.

Home was an uncomfortable place where four, soon to be six, people lived on top of each other in a one-bedroom apartment. There were rats on occasion, and during the sweltering summer months, bedbugs and other insects invaded his tiny oasis.

He glimpsed into the neighbor's apartment once. The space and the clean functional design were a stark contrast to the hallway lined with boxes of things on either side filled with food and things to be shipped home to St. Kitts and Jamaica.

The rest was clutter from the life his sister had had there for over ten years. She escaped to the suburbs of Baltimore, but his confinement seemed unending. Come to think of it, all the neighbors on his floor were new. Just the other day the ones next door moved out.

He never knew their names, but he remembered the young couple because the girl was the most beautiful Hispanic woman he had ever seen. She was very friendly, one of the few persons that ever said hello to him.

Her hellos were more welcomed than the nods of the drug dealer on the bottom floor, who he often passed in conference with his minions of customers and team of pushers. Not exactly the epiphany of organized crime, but still very much an annoyance.

The old lady told him how the police busted a whole bunch of people, years ago, after discovering that drugs were being sent via FedEx to the building frequently.

It was hard to swallow the realization that the walls next door would be painted a new color, the sinks, cupboards replaced, and all signs of filth and roaches removed to vie the next tenant. The work had already begun.

He glimpsed a trash bag filled with pieces of the material the walls were made of and spotted workers going in and out. He was tickled by the thought that George, the super, would have to mop the steps and front lobby to remove the stale stench of piss—left by either dogs or humans—that lingered there.

He climbed the steps and his nose reacted to the fleecing fresh scent of laundry coming from one of the apartments downstairs, a welcoming contrast. He hung his coat and surveyed the spread of things that littered the hallway, recalling how the paramedics couldn't carry a stretcher through for his roommate about a week ago.

He awoke that morning to the haunting sounds of a mother bawling, distraught and concerned for her son. Missy, the Jamaican lady he affectionately referred to as the "old lady", was in the bedroom rubbing oil all over his roommate. The roommate had been foaming at the mouth and shaking uncontrollably, all symptoms of a seizure, which he didn't remember when the paramedics came.

The roommate's body was limp and very heavy. He struggled to hold him up and a break in the tension arrived. He could hear and feel his roommate breathing, his mother's sobs becoming less and less frantic. The roommate left with the paramedics and he felt embarrassed by all the effort needed to get him out of the room and through the hallway.

He had adapted to his discomforts and the world outside those four walls had given him a lot. He had a routine now. What started as an excursion to Westchester Square and an inquiry about Bible study at the Methodist church (which stood there for over two-hundred years) turned into helping Ms. Dee dig up the back of the church to grow peas and cucumbers.

The thought triggered memories of when he and his cousins used to go to the mountains with his grandmother, who was a farmer. She'd died a month ago and though the tears fell, those memories transcended into what he was doing at the church garden.

Peace comes in pieces it seems.

So he walked to karate Wednesday nights and Saturday mornings, where he felt embarrassed by the sensei mentioning that he was a computer engineer, even though he was educated as one. The kids looked up to him there, so he walked the streets to get to his new family. These were his pieces.

Darting through the side streets one Tuesday morning, trying not to be late for the computer classes he taught for free at the church, he encountered new streets, a block that is atypical of what people thought the Bronx was—a "Manhattan-esque" spot in the middle of a neighborhood.

He liked these discoveries I suppose, because they caused him to slow down, to the point where he didn't feel like a droid in a city of millions.

Like that scene in *Gladiator,* when Russell Crowe was superimposed onto a field of grass with a flowing breeze and an image of his wife and son that drowned out all the noise and blood and hardship.

I suppose that's how he felt when he walked the streets of the Bronx, like he was coming home.

Are You Lonesome Tonight?

Mindy Matijasevic

Mary moved into the building when we were ten. She was Italian. She had a loud scary mom, a shy, awkward, overweight older brother named Ralph, and an Irish stepfather who drove a bus. Her window faced the front, so we were able to yell her name and ask her to come out to play.

Unlike ours, their apartment was spotless. I once saw her mom pick up a dust ball with her hand. I had never seen someone do that before.

Mary had her own room. Pink. White furniture. A canopy bed. I had none of those things. Although I thought I should be jealous, I wasn't. I knew I wouldn't feel good in their house.

Her mom enjoyed humiliating the children. Once, she called Mary and me into her kitchen where she was running her washing machine. She was washing mop heads, so the water coming out and into the sink was black. She pointed to the water and said that it was from Ralphie's underwear.

I was shocked because that seemed like something a mean kid at school would say. Your mom is supposed to try to make it better somehow. My mother was extremely nice, but she couldn't hold it together and as a result, at that age, I often felt humiliated. Our problems were different, though.

Mary and I would hula hoop in my house to Elvis Presley records. That's how we timed how long we could keep the hula hoop going. Next to each song listed on the label were the minutes and seconds it played.

I remember the day Mary came to my house in tears because Elvis Presley got married. She'd hoped he'd wait for her to grow up and marry her. Though I told her that he didn't even know we were there, she couldn't get past her heartbreak. I guess I knew better than to think a celebrity would come for me.

I had other problems.

Mary and her brother went to Catholic school. I went to the nearby public school. She hated having to wear a uniform. I hated having to wear my cousin Robin's hand-me-downs, whether I liked them or not.

My grandmother would yell, "Those are good clothes! Whattaya mean you don't like 'em? Those are from the good stores, not cheap junk! I can't afford that. You'll wear them!"

On Sundays, my grandpa rested upstairs in order to be able to make it through another week at work, where he had to stand all day on swollen legs. My grandma and mother were both home and not hospitalized, but had a hard time getting out of bed and doing regular things. It hadn't always been that way. I had witnessed much of the destruction.

My teenage aunt was a violent person and often had us terrorized. My other aunts, uncles, and cousins who lived in Queens, were not to know what went on in our house. Grandma warned me that they would break up her home, and I'd be put in a foster home where I'd be abused and no one would believe me.

In spite of their difficulties, my mother and grandparents tried very hard to spare me that fate. Mary and her brother went to be with their real father every Sunday. Most of the kids had family things to do.

I sat on the stoop, lonely and bored. I never met my father. Now that was something I envied. She had a real father. Every Sunday.

Untitled

B. Lawrence

My remembrances of life in the Bronx go back to when I was eight or nine and I used to go outside to play. The Forest Houses NYCHA housing development was across the street. There was a family, the Thomases, that we saw every day. The way they ate and talked and behaved fascinated me and my siblings. We'd stay there all day soaking up the atmosphere.

There were ten children—the mother was very heavy—and she burned an incense-like substance to help her with her breath, since she suffered from asthma. Today we talk a lot of persons being unhealthy in poor neighborhoods. Well, this was in the early 1960s and she made her apartment welcome to her children's friends.

Another memory is of the Brown family, whose mother had a husky voice that went up and down, from deep whiskey throat to a whisper. She also made her home welcome to the neighborhood children. Her kids had a schedule and her household had very specific rules. Never mind that it was summer and still light out.

The children had to go to bed and their friends had to leave—we didn't have that kind of routine. They lived on the top floor of a building on Westchester Avenue near 155th Street and were the first family I knew of who used the roof like their own private terrace.

We had always been told not to go on the roof, because that's where people were thrown off or assaulted. Mrs. Brown changed the whole way I thought of roofs—they were not intrinsically dangerous. How they were allowed to be used made them a threat or not. That was a happy time for me. I had to call my older sister for some of the details like addresses, but after fifty years, I remember those families.

The Bronx is different, and for me, a lot more impersonal. Relationships are fleeting and not very deep. It seems we have all adapted masks behind our economic and neighborhood prosperity. It has served as a place for me to get married, get divorced, raise two daughters, work for the city, obtain higher education degrees, retire, serve my community (including elective office) and keep going strong.

Mathland

Judy Bratnick

(with apologies to Edwin Abbott and Flatland)

Once upon a time, in a land not too far away, there lived a bunch of numbers and their ruler—the mathemagician. The mathemagician had an analytical mind, but he always remembered the Euclidean theorems and was correspondingly cautious. Now you might think that he had an easy time of it because numbers live in ordered sets, but that was not true of these numbers. Only the real, positive integers lived an orderly existence.

The irrational numbers were, of course, irrational and refused to be spoken to, but mumbled to themselves in an irritated sort of way. The imaginary numbers looked down upon everyone else and lived in their own land. The negative numbers displayed a negative attitude about any suggestion and refused to follow orders. The prime numbers associated with no one and kept to themselves.

Zero, of course, kept company with only itself and only rarely associated with any other number. And so it went.

Now you might think that the probability of all these problems existing at the same time was really very low, say $p<0,1$. But you would be mistaken. Once one set of numbers declaimed that they were special, all numbers also believed that they, too, were special. There was nothing normal about this distribution. In fact, the population of all numbers was indescribably difficult to manage.

Although when assembled into an ordered table, the resulting curve was both accurate and precise. The mathemagician, being young, had an interest in only the sorts of curves associated with women. You would be correct in assuming that all of this caused difficulty with certain functions.

Algebraic functions, being the snobs of the group, paid no attention to the mathemagician. Transcendental functions were uncooperative and followed no obvious rules at all. Natural log functions spent their days cursing out ln (e) although this made absolutely no sense at all. Meanwhile log 10 functions considered themselves to be superior and paid no mind to anyone else.

The most difficult of all were, of course, the complex numbers and the groups containing them required special handling. All the operators were up in arms because they, too, didn't know what to do with such intransigence. Even the commutative and associative laws were unequal to this situation.

"Oh what to do, what to do," moaned the mathemagician.

It was then that he realized that his numbers knew no limits, and being a surly lot, required discipline. He decided to set limits, ranges, and domains for all the population. But first he had to get everyone's attention. This was a complicated undertaking especially because the sets, groups, and fields required and demanded special treatment.

"The logical thing to do," said the mathemagician to himself, "is to tackle each problem separately."

And so he did. First, he gave Thorazine to the irrational numbers which made them more in touch with reality. Then he pulled the real positive integers aside and said, "You are an infinitely large group and I will treat you that way in the future." This made them far more cooperative than they had been in the past.

The imaginary numbers were issued visas allowing them to work in Mathland. They were pleased but puzzled. "We have always been around or hadn't you noticed?" they said. When they heard about this, the complex numbers, which had always exhibited a certain sort of snobbery (because they, of course, had real components), became more down to earth and seemed pleased.

The prime numbers were reassured that their special circumstances were well understood and were encouraged to learn from their peers. They began speaking to the irrational numbers, which having taken Thorazine, were mumbling to themselves, but seemed pleased with this initiative—although both groups knew that they had nothing in common.

As for the negative numbers, the mathemagician told them that he would multiply each by itself, thus destroying their negative attitude (although he was unsure if this would completely eradicate the problem). Zero was unique, but could be managed without allowing it to be too divisive. So, did they all live happily ever after?

Well, some numbers did.

As for the mathemagician—having a tendency to worry—he made a great effort to be happy. He noticed that the ellipses were becoming envious of the circles and were trying to make certain that their focal points all converged on a single point. Additionally, the hyperbolas felt left out and, as a consequence, spent much time berating the parabolas.

How this was resolved is a tale for another time.

The Accident

Paul Torres

On March 5, 2007 I had an accident that would change my life. It was a Monday. The first day of my work week. I woke all right, at around 8:30 a.m., took a shower, dressed, and ate breakfast. I lived in Park Slope, Brooklyn, a gentrified neighborhood. In one of the few rent-stabilized buildings left in the neighborhood; two blocks from Prospect Park. It's a beautiful part of Brooklyn.

I worked for a law firm in midtown Manhattan. I'd go two blocks to the Grand Army Plaza station and take either the #2 or #3 train to Penn Station, on 34th Street and 7th Avenue. I'd done this thousands of times before, as I'd been with the firm for over twenty-one years.

The firm was Milberg, LLP. My department, the file department, was on the 49th floor of 1 Penn Plaza, which is directly above Penn Station. I would get off the train and take an escalator to the lobby of 1 Penn Plaza. In order to take the elevator to my floor I had to use an ID card, thanks to post-September 11th security measures.

That morning I took a #3 train. I got off the train at Penn Station and lost consciousness. I had a seizure, which forced me onto the tracks of the subway. I gained consciousness about fifteen seconds later. The next few seconds saved my life. As I got a sense of where I was I decided to move my body to the middle of the track.

I'll never forget the feeling of being on the subway tracks. They are smelly, wet, and dirty! I don't recall if I called out for help. Once I made it to the middle of the tracks I sensed the rumbling sound of an arriving train. I had seconds to brace for the arriving #2 train.

I was on the end of the line so the train took what felt like minutes to pass over me. Then it stopped. It didn't move to leave the station. I braced for the motion of the gears, but it just stayed in the station. Eventually I heard people around me. Time seemed to stop when I was under there.

"Are you all right?"

"Are you hurt?"

I said I was okay.

There were about six people surrounding the bottom carriage of the train. Surrounding me. The crews of police and fire department emergency personnel were trying to figure out how to get me out of the situation. I can't remember what they said but the tone of their voices was reassuring.

Looking at myself later in newspaper photos in the station you can see a brace on my neck. They immobilized my head with tape and gave me intravenous fluids. They put an oxygen mask on me and I was shirtless. It's funny thinking about it now, but I was absolutely calm when I was on the tracks. Can't explain why. Maybe it's my personality.

I've always reacted calmly in situations which are stressful.

The Fall Classic and the South Bronx

Edgar E. Cabrera

I cherish the fond memories experienced on my multifarious Park Avenue city block in the South Bronx. My apartment complex was such an impressionable edifice it still feels displaced to me. Our beautifully-designed courtyard was superior to that of other housing projects in the neighborhood, a well-planned and aesthetically-pleasing layout, including stone seating installations, tall trees for climbing, balcony hallways reminiscent of Florida hotels.

It was our own fun house and safe haven.

María López Plaza, as our building was called, shared the block with an open parking lot and two undeveloped gated grass fields. All spaces used by my friends and I when playing our American sports and children games. I loved the summer as a child. My block was visited by popup events such as carnivals, circuses, and evangelist missionary parties—all finding temporary residence in empty lots scattered throughout the summer.

My father, Edgar V. Cabrera, served as the highly sought after, oftentimes lifesaving superintendent, for the first twenty-eight years of the building's existence. Growing up on that high traffic street in my South Bronx ghetto was all I ever knew. That was until the day our hometown New York Yankees beat the Atlanta Braves to reclaim their inveterate position as World Champions. I witnessed the Bronx Bombers' legacy of global dominance in baseball reign hope over our adjoining impoverished city district.

Watching the Yankees play in the fall classic became a theme in my childhood, growing up in the 1990s, and this was to be my induction along with our new dynastic team. When the Yankees won Game 6 of the 1996 World Series, Yankee Stadium became my own version of Willy Wonka's Chocolate Factory—filled with Cracker Jacks, Ball Park franks, little bat boys playing Oompa Loompas, bleacher creatures, box seats for the city's elite, and twenty-two World Championships that promulgated our infamy as the most celebrated team in professional sports.

The old stadium, often referred to as "The House That Ruth Built," was a paragon for sporting venues, and us locals who'd never been inside often fantasized of the wondrous moments that must've taken place there.

The Yankees had not won a championship in close to twenty years and fans desperately wanted The Bombers to bring this one home. The game's precedence generated an excitement on the street, a delightful atmosphere only comparable to Nuyorican hype leading up to Parade Day.

The Puerto Rican flag and the NY Yankees logo were the first things I identified with living in the Bronx. These symbols have defined me as a person since I was young. An American through affiliation and a champion by design. The game was the only subject of conversation entertained at the bodega. The drunkards who loitered inside the establishment had placed wagers on the game and were louder than usual.

Bronxites crossed the street from the corner store carrying cases of Coors Light and Budweiser, huge bottomless bags of Cheeze Doodles and Dipsy Doodles, 3-liter bottles of the then popular Pepsi and 7 Up.

Come game time my brother, who is eight years my senior, sixteen at the time, was searching for a better place to spend his evening, ideally in bedrooms of nearby females while their fathers were bound to baseball.

"Yo bro, I'm going to watch the game across the street. Tell ma I'll be back," Seco said, with an indifferent attitude.

"I think papi's planning to have people over to watch the game," I said, with a hopeful plea.

"I'll be back to celebrate after the game's over."

With that he ran off into the jungle to enjoy his reckless teenage lifestyle.

My father, "El Súper", sensed the magnitude of this game, and knew if the Yankees won, it could lead to an overwhelmingly huge celebration—like those all-night dance parties we hosted every New Year's Eve. The amount of food, drinks, and cleanup that came along with those gatherings was not something we hoped to sponsor that weekend.

Instead of having an uncontrollable amount of neighbors come inside our home to watch the game, using civic ingenuity, my dad decided to bring the television outside and have people gather on the street. It was unconventional to us children at first, but we fantasized about future video game tournaments that would happen in the same outdoor TV fashion.

As word spread, neighborhood faces began congregating in front of our ground level apartment. My father continued about his setup while neighbors speculated.

"C'mon Súper, do your job and provide us poor folk with a TV to watch," said one.

"How are we supposed to watch the game on that tiny screen?" said another.

"Where's the arroz con gandules?"

My father, the building's maintenance guru, used the always dependable industrial-strength orange extension cord that supplied life to all block parties, and lugged our television set outside for all the neighborhood folk to watch.

Papi turned it on and we listened to the announcer call the game, watching all the stars like Bernie Williams, Andy Petitte, Mariano Rivera, and Derek Jeter, becoming living legends and names that would live on in history.

After the game ended with the Yankees on top of the world, I saw faces who had trouble finding a reason to smile, others erupting in cheers. Neighbors came out of their apartments to join those already on 151st Street, to come together as a community chanting "Let's go Yankees!"

My brother Seco returned carrying a bunch of value brand sodas in colorful flavors and distributed them amongst our friends, as if it were our prize for winning. He shook his bottle and busted it open, mimicking what the Yankee players did on TV with bottles of champagne.

He sprayed soda in every direction, adding color to our lives, ensuring this moment would live on, to one day elicit Bronx nostalgia.

Feel the Beat

Sarah Smith

I'm a born-and-bred Manhattan girl at heart, but for the last thirteen years, my feet have moved daily to the rhythms of the Bronx. A little salsa, merengue, I have the moves. A little wining, soca, and I can shake it with the best. But play that old school hip hop and "I move to the rhythms of the boogie-d-beat".

My first trip to the Bronx was in the 70s, when I was on a second double date with one of my younger sisters. My sister was a tall, light-skinned female with wavy Indian hair and thick legs, descendant of South Cakalack-key redbones and Georgia red dirt backwoods.

Her date was a tall high-yella brother, we called JV. Hyped, loud with a reddish-brown afro, crazy funny and likable. He had a short darker-skinned older brother and I was the short darker-skinned older sister.

I spent my first year at a college upstate, and was now a college student back home with my family. He was a high school dropout with a Ph.D. in street life, who'd just come home from a year on an island, Riker's Island, that is. But he was cute, polite and fun.

We both loved music and loved to dance.

Riding the subway uptown to the Bronx was exciting, scary, and brand new. We were from Manhattan's Westside, you know, the 100s and Broadway. We generally rode the train downtown or visited relatives in Long Island or New Jersey.

Back then, if you weren't going to work or visiting a relative, you didn't go to certain neighborhoods, and the Bronx had a reputation all its own.

Denim jacket and jeans. A tube top, with a bra underneath. I was a little top-heavy for some of my moves, and I figured I would fit right in. My sister who was in love, did not care about the latest style.

Soon we were in the Bronx, walking past a bodega, barber shop and botanica. Walking through the projects, we reached a section of space near the basketball court where a table held a couple of turntables with nearby speakers. A string of extension cords reached up into a window. It was hot out and the benches were full of the old and young. Strollers, some kids on roller-skates and bikes, a pickup game on the court, and us, standing around waiting for the music to start.

Shy and just a little nervous, I didn't like crowds. I had never hung out on the grounds of the projects in Manhattan, visiting my friends in their apartments or waiting in the hallway. Or they'd come to my house, hang in front of my building, or head down to Riverside Park.

We didn't' know anyone except the two brothers we were with, and were a long way from home to get lost. It was strange going into an unknown neighborhood with someone you just started seeing. You didn't know anything about their history or baggage, so you needed to be on alert. But JV and Tiny seemed to be well known, and while I caught people checking us out, we didn't get any static from anyone.

I felt like we had been out there too long and anything could jump off. I turned to my sister to discuss leaving, and the music started playing. *Mamase mamasa mamakusa.* And there was the beat, the beat, repetitious, echoing on two turntables, and I was moving, body shaking, thighs quaking, moving to the beat.

A little Manu Dibango, TSOP with "Love is the Message", anything James Brown, and I was getting down. Yes, the music was playing/bodies swaying and if you knew the words to the song, everybody sang along. Suddenly, I didn't care where I was, or who was with me. I was lost in the music and the songs kept starting over and over, building and we were tensed, waiting for the hook.

The DJ took his time getting there.

And just when I thought I couldn't take it anymore, like being brought to the edge of an orgasm, body wet, soaking wet, breathless and tired and dripping in sweat, then came the hook. And I was down, in a squat, feet kicking out from under me like a Russian dancer, rising up/down, on the beat.

Fast, faster, picking up the pace, I rose up, arms swaying, moving to the horns, my butt following the drums and my head rocking to the keyboard, and the next song was whispering through the background and I hollered 'oh shit, that's my jam'. You know I wanted to rest, but I kept on dancing.

Someone on the mic started rhyming and everyone kicked in with a call and response. *And it's on and on, and on and on, like hot butter on the what? POPCORN!*

Keep on and you don't stop. It's the rhythm that makes your body rock.

Wow. The little playground was turned out.

As darkness fell, the street lights came on. Somebody held a flashlight near the turntables, and old folks gathered little children and headed upstairs to hot apartments with a fan, and ice in a metal cup. Outside someone passed a soda, or a beer, and Kool cigarettes was the smoke of choice. The party played on and on, 'til the break of dawn.

And we stayed, my sister sitting on a bench with JV's arms around her, and Tiny and I still dancing on the asphalt. Then daylight arrived and like creatures of the night, everyone started to creep away, and we shuffled our tired feet, clinging clothes on damp bodies, to the train station, in the coolness of the morning breeze.

We stood on the platform, watching the morning unfold to the beat of the Bronx, and listening for the rhythm of the train to take us back to Manhattan.

First Christmas

Hayley Camacho

The dishes were done and the dining table sparkled from just being polished. I felt satisfied, industrious. It was about 1:00 p.m. and the afternoon stretched ahead with no definite plan.

"You're going in today?" I asked Eddie

"Yeah, sorry," he said. "Henry has us working like crazy to get these drawings done for this new client next week. It'll just be for a few hours. I'll be back by 4 o'clock or so. We can go to a movie later," he added, smiling.

"I think I'll go to Woolworths and buy some Christmas decorations and ornaments," I said. "Maybe tomorrow we can go buy a tree."

"You know, there's a little store near our office," he said. "We could go there and take a look at the trees."

It was the first weekend in December and I was excited about Christmas—our first Christmas together.

We kissed goodbye and went our separate ways. Once outside, I realized I had bundled up a little too much. The temperature had not yet dipped to the extreme lows of winter, the sky was a crystal blue. I was in good spirits, walking along our block of solid pre-war buildings and up the hill past the dry cleaner and supermarket.

Slightly off in the distance, I could see the brown brick buildings of Parkchester. They looked like the skyline of a separate little city. Many of the buildings had sculptures of people on the exteriors—mothers with young children, men laboring, even clowns.

I crossed the busy intersection and entered the main shopping area on East Avenue. I passed Womraths, the bookstore where I went with my brother in the eighth grade, to buy a copy of *Of Mice and Men*. Next to that was the Selby shoe store. I loved those stores. The lettering on the signs was a 1950s/1960s font. It made me feel like I was back in time.

Salvation Army volunteers rang their bells in front of Macys and passersby tossed their coins or placed bills in the iron till that hung from a tripod. I walked past and crossed the street over to Woolworths. I began browsing on the street level. I always went to the cosmetic section, looking at bottles of Cover Girl "clean" makeup, Angel Face pressed powders and blushes, and Maybelline eye shadows in various hues.

Mod 60s fashions had made a comeback and I examined bangle bracelets of varying widths in the jewelry area. I purchased fuchsia pink and lime green bangles to go with a black, striped tunic dress that was one of my favorite things to wear to work. Pleased with my ability to accessorize for the New Wave look, I proceeded downstairs to choose some ornaments for our first Christmas tree.

I couldn't help take a detour from the Christmas section to go to the pet care section and admire the canaries in pastel shades of yellow, green and blue. Then it was back to my destination.

Bins in the center of the floor glittered with packs of silver and blue tinsel, next to stiff-looking garland. There were boxes of blue, red, green and pink glass ornaments, some frosted with white glitter. Those caught my eye.

Growing up, the ornaments on our silver tinsel tree were red and white satin-covered balls, which would never break. Glass ornaments were elegant, classic, like the ornaments on Christmas trees from films and TV shows of the 1960s. I picked up several boxes. I also picked up a little Santa ornament and a happy little mouse on skis, which still gets placed at the very top of our tree.

The next day Eddie and I drove to Mamaroneck. We had lunch on the main street and then walked over to the household goods shop. It was a no-frills store. There was a four-foot tree on display and we told the salesperson we wanted to buy it. She went to the back and brought out an appropriately-sized box.

I couldn't wait to set up and start decorating our first tree when we got home. Eddie got a small knife from the kitchen and sliced through the tape at the top of the box. He pulled out a small box from the top. We both thought it was the stand. He opened it up and inside was a small tree, about two feet tall. We looked at each other puzzled.

He pulled out the next box and opened it to find another little tree. There were four more tiny trees and we started to laugh.

"Hey I could make a little money," he said. "I could sell these on the corner and make a quick sixty bucks."

I laughed so hard, tears rolled down my cheeks.

The next day, we got into our green Datsun and went back to Mamaroneck to return the little trees. Then we drove to JC Penney. Before paying, we asked the salesperson to open the box so we could double-check our tree.

My Dad was a Teamster Man, Not a Social Worker…and Yet…

Colleen Boris

Mom died in 1989. Dad, now living alone, often continued the weekly trips to the German butcher shop on Jerome Avenue to buy his sandwich meat for the following seven days or so.

This one warm afternoon, leaving the store with his small bag of bologna, salami, turkey breast and half a Kielbasa, he noticed a heavy set young Puerto Rican woman begging for money.

He approached her and offered to feed her. Off they walked, jaywalking across Jerome Avenue, under the #4 train, to a Greek diner.

I'll never know what Miriam told him during that meal—or how she told him. Whatever she said prompted Dad—a retired Teamster, high school graduate, not a psychiatrist, a social worker, a drug counselor and not a priest—to suggest to this self-described homeless drug addict that she needed a change of scenery.

Miriam's two children were taken away from her by the courts and she was living on the streets. And that is quite simply how Miriam came to live in Lodi, New Jersey. She moved into my father's 60' x 17' humble, clean and safe, mobile home. For the next four-and-a-half years, Miriam tried getting off the drugs. The whole time, Dad left his door open for her to come and stay with him. His only requirement was that she not be high.

To say my older sisters were concerned is like saying that Barbra Streisand can carry a tune. At first, my sister Joanne was apoplectic. She was understandably scared, worried, suspicious and angry. She felt it was our duty to intervene. Kathy was worried, of course, but she remained quiet about it.

Me? My attitude was this: Dad raised me to think for myself. He trusted me from a very early age to make my own decisions. Every time I asked Dad for advice about something, he would listen and say, "I can't tell you what to do. You know what's best for you."

Although that was not always true, the simple reassurance and confidence he showed in my judgment made me able to make decisions for myself. It also allowed me to deal with the consequences of my own actions and not create scapegoats for any regrettable decisions. That freedom to decide for myself has served me well throughout my life.

I had to give Dad the same respect and freedom. Even if Miriam robbed him, hurt him, God forbid, killed him, I was willing to risk it. That deeply rooted mutual love and respect for each other's inner voice was alive and well.

Dad's outer voice, meanwhile, was teaching Miriam many basic simple things about life. He taught her how to shop, how to reach to the back of the shelf for the latest expiration dates. He showed her how to look for sales and use coupons. He taught her how to cook inexpensive meals and how to do laundry.

He taught her how to relax in her own skin. Eventually, Miriam got clean. It took a few years and it wasn't a smooth road but she persevered and finally was able to live without the pull of the drugs. She went to family court and DCS and regained custody of her kids.

She found an apartment in the Bronx.

By this time, her younger daughter, Emily, had become as much a part of my family as my nieces and nephews. Emily was about four when she met my dad and she was a year younger than Joanne's daughter, Rebecca.

Holidays were often spent at my family gatherings. Once they moved back to the Bronx, I expected we'd never see them again.

I was mistaken. My generous sister Joanne paid for a taxi to take Miriam and Emily to New Jersey almost every Saturday afternoon. They would spend the day grocery shopping at the local supermarkets, which had (and have) much better prices than any in New York City. Miriam's food stamps had more buying power there. On Sunday, they went home again via taxi, thanks to Joanne.

This continued for about three more years. The visits stopped rather suddenly. Miriam had met a man. She told my father, but not right away. Even though Dad's relationship with Miriam was platonic, I guess this man did not understand.

My dad was angry and hurt. Not because she met a man. No, he was mad because Miriam lied to him. While my sister and my father were helping Miriam by giving her a little money each week, Miriam was already living with this man and was no longer in need of Dad's generosity.

She stopped coming around. She never called, never wrote, and we never heard from them again. Dad died in 2011. There was no way of knowing whether she saw his obituary in the *New York Daily News* or not.

Emily would be twenty-four now. I sometimes wonder what memories, if any, she has of my father. He was like a grandfather to her for almost seven years during her early childhood.

Someone suggested that maybe the reason we never heard from them is because Miriam went back on drugs. I choose not to believe that.

I am a Tattooed Woman

Sidra Lackey

I became a tattooed woman at the age of twenty-five. But if I had my way I would have been a tattooed teen. The only reason I didn't is because to get a tattoo, even if you were eighteen, you needed a state ID card (or a parent present) and I was without one when I inquired about the design I hoped to get at the time. By the time I got an ID I was no longer intensely interested in getting a tattoo.

The tattoo I wanted when I was a teenager was Betty Boop or my name. Fast forward to 2011, I got my Betty tattoo, and in 2013 my name (well in a sense, I got the meaning of it, "star", in the image of a star). The first tattoo shop I visited, Tuff City in the Bronx, New York, was where I hoped to get my first tattoo when I was just a teen.

I returned in 2010 and got a tattoo there (my 15th at the time).

I didn't plan to get tattooed at twenty-five. In my teens, when I craved ink, it was more because of the fad of tattoos prevalent in the 90s. I wanted in. At age twenty-five I decided to become tattooed for personal reasons. My first tattoo was a lock and the reason behind it was personal. I chose the form of a tattoo to express my feelings behind the lock (rather than buying a lock necklace) because I felt the permanence of a tattoo really cemented that strong feeling.

And I feel that way about some tattoos, that don't have deep meaning (they're fun or aesthetically pleasing to me), I've gotten after my first. I would have never predicted after my first tattoo, I'd keep going under the needle. I admit I am addicted to them. I don't foresee myself stopping my collection because there will always be a time in my life where I will want to get a tattoo to tell about it.

You can definitely tell someone is an enthusiast if they have more tattoos than their age. I have gotten (yet again, at Tuff City, one of my favorite tattoo shops) my 37th—Edgar Allan Poe's signature. And I already have in mind my next couple—a vintage perfume bottle, Catwoman, maybe another Michael Jackson tribute, and one dedicated to my affection for Britney Spears' music.

I plan to make a pilgrimage soon enough to New Orleans to get tattooed by the first known African American woman tattoo artist, Jacci Gresham, who works at Aart Accent. I'm ecstatic to be tattooed by such a legend. I've mused that maybe I will let her pick a design for me—something that she sees fits me.

But I'm leaning towards having her tattoo the phrase 'Tattooed Woman' with her signature or initials under it. I also plan to trek to New Zealand to get worked on by an artist who specializes in traditional Maori tattoo art (or Ta moko) that I'm curious about.

Being a tattooed woman has been an interesting journey thus far. The positives are that I get to wear beautiful, cool, meaningful art on me, and that my tattoos make me feel more confident—the fact that I chose to look different through permanent body modification is empowering.

The negatives are the sometimes undesirable comments and looks I get because I am a woman (especially because I'm a black woman), where tattoos aren't accepted widely by the community and particularly on women, or the stigma that because I am tattooed I am anything from easy to uneducated, hardly the case.

The positives outweigh the negatives, however.

If I had the option of having all my tattoos magically removed, I wouldn't do it. I adore them and would not be me without them. They make me more me. I say it loud: I am a tattooed woman, I am meant to be a tattooed woman, and I am proud to be a tattooed woman.

Little Things

Ranjit K. Sahu

An addition to the family is always a joy, yet her entry into the household was an experience that made the Bronx special forever. A little being may not occupy much space in the expanse of the Bronx, yet she singly changed the way we looked at it.

It would be close to eight years since our first acquaintance with the Bronx neighborhood, the people, the birds and squirrels, the trees and the changing colors of the seasons, when one spring about a couple of years back, we allowed her to creep into our lives. The first time she stepped inside our house we awaited her to open her eyes and take note of her new home, and her new family. It was not until two days later that panic set in when we realized she never opened her eyes throughout the days.

"Something is pretty wrong with her. At least she should respond to our voices," the lady of the house said, with an air of certain knowledge.

We were ready with a name for her and were just waiting to call her by that name and see her respond. It was a wait like that of a mother or nurses waiting for the baby to cry aloud, to announce her arrival. The third day we could not sleep, and late after sunset, we saw her twist a little. And then she woke up as if startled by our presence.

"Vanilla," I said softly.

She turned her head and looked straight into my eyes, as if acknowledging her new identity. In a few moments she moved and we realized the folly we had made. We had expected her to sleep and wake up like us. She wouldn't, she had her own timetable.

It was soon a routine to see her run around the house and accept food and also let us touch her and play with her. The initial unfamiliarity had now been transformed to a bond of unexplained passions. She responded to my call even though I never heard her voice. Her eyes, however, expressed whatever she could not speak. She was the indispensable part of the family.

Her life had entangled with a small fraction of our lives, yet she had made that small period of life worthwhile. She had entered our lives and would stay on forever in our memories, even though she left our world a couple of years later.

The squirrels still scurry across grassy lawns of the Bronx and birds still sing their arrival. Yet somewhere in the untold silence of our home, the Bronx had been given a new meaning to a family of immigrants.

Vanilla had made us a part of the Bronx and we got associated with the borough through her, for it was through her in the Bronx that we realized that things, however small, had a way of connecting you to the vast mystic dimensions of creation.

"A love for life and all things living" was a new motto that a little hamster had given us.

And her fond memories help make the Bronx a special place for us.

Webster Avenue and Nearby

Jose Quiles

When I was four years old my parents rented a room on Brook Avenue and 167th Street. They shared this 10' x 15' room with my two siblings. The bathroom and kitchen were outside in the hall and were shared by other tenants on the landing. It was a five-story walkup. We shared a bed with cockroaches and I remember going outside to play and getting hit by a police cruiser.

Several years later we moved to a five-room apartment in the same neighborhood. The landlord, Mr. Rivera, was Cuban. He maintained the building well, even putting a lace curtain over the window on the top of the front door, which was never locked. He and my parents were good friends.

The neighborhood was safe, everyone knew each other, and people played dominoes and cards outside. I played with the other children until nine or ten at night in the summer. When I got older, I learned how to smoke cigarettes with my neighbor Norris in the backyard.

Across the street there were more tenement buildings. By the time I was fourteen things were starting to change. Some of those buildings were empty and others burned to the ground. The fire trucks were a constant in the neighborhood. Every day we would smell the scent of burning wood. When the buildings were no longer livable, the city stepped in and turned them into projects.

That's when heroin became more visible, soon destroying lives and families.

People would go into the projects to cop and take the dope to the empty buildings next door to shoot up. They would wander out nodding on street corners or on benches in the park nearby. Little by little, people in the neighborhood stopped going to the park. Landlords like ours started installing solid wooden doors with deadbolts—no more glass panels, curtains, or open doors.

Mom and pop stores started getting robbed and one by one closed up. No new businesses moved in. But I always found ways to make some money. I carried groceries home for customers at the A & P on 167th Street and Morris

Avenue, and babysat a neighbor's kids. She and her husband had separated and she had to go to work. I had known the couple for years. They were about fifteen years older than I was and I thought of Georgie, the husband, as an older brother. He came around every couple of weeks to see the kids.

One night he invited me to go to a party with him in Harlem.

When we got there, he introduced me around and everybody was friendly, offering beer, liquor, and cigarettes. I sat back and took it all in. I was sixteen and it was the first adult party I had been to. I noticed people going into another room, coming out looking different. They'd come out rubbing their noses, eyes half closed, then sit down and relax into a nod.

Georgie was one of them.

So I decided to go in and see what it was all about. I sat down on the floor, noticing a glass of water with several syringes in it next to me. People were shooting up. Someone asked me if I had ever done it before, if I wanted to try it. I was curious so I said yes and they skin popped me. I immediately threw up. But after a while a calm sensation came over me and I sat in the living room nodding with everyone else.

After a couple of hours Georgie took me home. I went straight to bed so my parents wouldn't notice anything. From then on, I watched the activity going on at the project across the street. When I saw someone I knew going over there I'd ask them to take me with them so I could cop, too. At that point you had to know somebody to score.

Before long I was known to the dealers and could go on my own. I was using every day. I was a functioning addict. I continued going to school for another year, but when my girlfriend got pregnant I quit. We got married and I went to work. She didn't know I was using at first but eventually found out.

For a while everything was fine.

As long as I had my fix I was able to work, have a family life, take my kids on trips to the park for picnics, to museums, to see family. When the kids got sick we took them to the hospital. But as time went on my habit increased and I spent more and more time trying to get enough money to buy my poison. Along with other users I'd run the streets chasing stronger dope—we'd hear about some powerful heroin arriving, that several people had OD'd on it, and we'd run to the spot to get it.

At that time there was no Narcan, so ODs were common. I don't know how many birthdays, holiday dinners, and other important family functions I missed. Now I scream in silence at the opportunities I lost behind my heroin use. Thank God, towards the end, I discovered syringe exchange, so I at least avoided contracting HIV.

I became a syringe exchange worker myself. I learned about Narcan and was able to bring people out of overdoses several times. Today I still have a habit—methadone—but at least I'm not running the streets putting myself at risk.

I have become a peer counselor at my methadone clinic educating people about Hepatitis C. Some of my kids keep in touch with me and I am so happy they still want to have a relationship with me. I don't make any excuses for the choices I made. I'm just glad that now I can make a small contribution helping others.

Undocumented

Peggy Robles-Alvarado

My historical facts are unpleasant. That's why I didn't take any pictures after the age of fifteen. Well, I did pose for pictures on rare occasions, but I let the Kodak film pile up in the top drawer of my dresser, undeveloped. That way my family couldn't complain that I didn't observe the tradition of documenting their granddaughter's infamous first birthday, where the birthday girl cried at the sight of all the unfamiliar faces, sweats out her poufy pink dress of lace and tulle, and vomits after overdosing on cake icing.

There are no photos of me past the age of fifteen because I was never really able to be sixteen, seventeen, eighteen, or nineteen. I didn't have the customary Sweet Sixteen celebration easing me into womanhood. No sign of my father's clumsy changing of the ballet flat to a pinky toe crushing high heel shoe.

No tearful mother bestowing the title of mujer on her youngest child with the gentle placing of the tiara over my salon blowout. No prom pictures to show off my seventeen-year-old self in a twenty-dollar knockoff little black dress from Third Avenue or the absence of a date. No one was interested in dating the Hester Prynne of John F. Kennedy High School.

I was an embodiment of contradictions, too much to consider for the average teenage boy. Eventually, I decided to attend the "Out The Door in '94" prom after a friend convinced me that joining her and her boyfriend wouldn't make me a third wheel. Later that night, I learned my presence in the limo served two very important purposes. First, they had someone to split the bill with and second, I was a living example of why she wanted to remain a virgin that night.

So from fifteen I went straight to twenty-one—womanhood *al expreso*. Who wants to capture the dark circles and bags under your eyes after endless late night feedings and cramming for A.P. English?

Parenting while still a high school student in a gifted and talented program (just waiting for your grade point average to drop below an 82 so they can finally get rid of the eyesore that threatens their funding) left little time or desire for snapping pictures of the self. Why bother? Why keep a record of this past when immediate family, distant relatives who had heard "the news" and friends (who were not really friends) wouldn't let me forget it?

Besides, engorged breasts and milk stains appearing on my only United Colors of Benetton t-shirt during microbiology caused permanent frown lines like the ones middle aged women get when they discover their husbands are cheating on them. My boobs deceived me each day around the same time as Ms. Forester began explaining the lab procedure for the day. Those painful leaking enemies of the State, defied nursing pads, wads of napkins and branded any cute top (that I had purchased with the intent of just looking like every other girl in my class) with the mark of motherhood.

Leche! No need for photos.

The only reason one photo of my high school graduation even exists is because our neighbor Minerva came by after the ceremony and insisted I pose for a picture with my mom and daughter. She fussed on and on about this being a milestone—that graduating with the rest of my class despite having made such a grave mistake in welcoming motherhood so soon was a show of effort on my part, and the result of my mother's support.

She added that my mother could have done what her sister Lila did when her daughter decided to abrir las patas muy temprano and send her off to live in Santiago. But no! My mother was brave for standing by me. She might as well have been a martyr. Canonized for how well she handled all the bochinche! She did the best she could, Minerva sighed, pero mala hierba crece aunque uno no quiera.

My mother held my daughter as we all stared blankly at the camera like the photos of wet nurses in the 1800s I had studied in Mr. Tubman's class. This too seemed endless and uncomfortable. Minerva took my cap and placed it on the baby's head, positioned the tassel, smiled and affirmed that she would be smarter than I was.

We held our unaffectionate gazes trying to hide the undercurrent of shame that marked my family. But shame is palpable. It glows in front of the camera telling its own lucid story even if you flash a smile or wrap yourself around your mom's arm for the first time in seven months. Documenting our faces that day made it undeniable—I was the sinvergüenza Malinche of the family.

The Kodak proved it.

Uncle Brodus

Dale Benjamin Drakeford

The red clay, hard and hot as a biscuit left out a second noon in August, slapped his bare feet to know pain that no longer bothered him. His troublemaking kin, teasing the law just short of a hanging, would not blemish his mood—they didn't bother him either. They were just being who they be, but you know these otters bit up yonder.

"Nice. Real nice."

"Don't you think they nice?"

The day of hauling logs and picking cotton was commonplace, not uncommon labor at all. He was tired, that deep in the bone where the skeleton bruises kind of tired, but he still had a kind word, or none at all, for all who crossed his path.

"Nice. Isn't he nice?"

"Sure is nice," he said, for his nephew to hear of a fellow pedestrian fetching him an invite to well water.

Uncle Brodus was jello yellow where bleached orange meets off-white. He was ready jolly with a smile from big toe hangnail to curly brown locks holding back pre-midlife balding. He never met a pig he didn't see as bacon or a person he didn't call "neighbor."

Uncle Brodus loved his brothers the way triceps love strong knee muscles. They worked together, played together and thought thoughts together as if attached by brain synapses and not just blood. Their arguments were like beer fests where jokes were the commodity and serious banter the timeout segment. If the brothers were additional limbs and extended good life, the sisters were princesses on extended leave from royal duties but not royal respect.

Uncle Brodus was a father of nine. His eight daughters were his heart and his only son, the baby boy that came at the end, "Junior," his reward for showing his girls love, not how much he wanted that boy. He knew himself to be a good person, accepted that others saw it every day, and took what came his way as the blessing his goodness bought.

Asthma came his way and he was thankful for the "mist that followed in glorious invention." The handheld spray was his reward, the asthma nothing but an inconvenience.

Ratcliff

N.D. Ratcliff

While the Boogie Down Bronx is gearing up for festivities to celebrate its centennial, I've been working feverishly on my memoir. It's been bittersweet. Extremely homesick, I love my family, but they don't all love me.

Growing up, I was raised in a cult, but you couldn't tell Momma that. She always said, "If you don't serve Jehovah you can't live in my house!"

Beautiful with a mean streak, modest, respectable, and never one to get involved in politics or drama, Momma lived to serve Jehovah. Momma met Lee, my dad, just after ninth grade, at a gathering for Jehovah Witnesses and bore him four children.

Lee was raised by his Creole mom, a Jehovah's Witness, and Spanish stepfather. His father Ratcliff was absent. Lee was a senior, on the verge of graduating, until the school discovered that he didn't have enough credits. Lee and a friend came up with a plan during the madness of the 1971 San Fernando earthquake that registered 6.6 on the Richter scale, and breaking into L.A. High School, he stole his diploma.

We resided at the foothills of the San Gabriel Valley Mountains in Altadena, California, where we enjoyed tranquil hiking trails, horses, and hidden waterfalls. But the other side of this rural paradise offered Santa Ana winds, brush fires, flooding and mudslides.

Our first home was right next to NASA's Jet Propulsion Laboratory. We didn't celebrate any holidays. But during Christmas, Momma enjoyed driving us up and down Christmas Tree Lane on Santa Rosa Avenue. Viewing the colorful well-lit hundred-year-old Deodara cedar trees made me green with envy that Santa Claus never visited our home.

Momma and dad's relationship was disastrous, lasting for nine years. Mom could no longer bare him neglecting us, and sleeping with the neighbor—especially after the bastard was born. Full of rage, she picked up the family gun and let off a few rounds at daddy, missing him, but destroying the television.

She divorced Lee, which caused him great agony.

To soothe his pain he drank often. Dad had been given the bottle since he was a baby. The first photograph of him, he was less than two years old and clutching a large bottle of Four Roses bourbon. Ms. Josephine, his French Creole grandmother, would babysit him and tow him to the local bars where he was given the French nickname "Cochon", or pig.

In July of 1982, when I was five, while R&B star Evelyn Champagne King was making her "Love Come Down" on the country, Lee died from cirrhosis of the liver. But my Grandma Jean, his mom, swore up and down that my mom killed him, because he drank to forget about her.

I remembered him kindly. Walking into the Kingdom Hall of Jehovah's Witnesses while holding his hand. Sitting next to him. He had on all gray and his hair was cornrowed, looking strong and confident. Being at his wake and watching him while he slept, I had no idea where he was heading. He looked peaceful. I wanted him to wake up, but he refused.

Momma didn't go to the funeral and I always wondered what it would have been like to have a father.

Dad was buried at Valhalla Cemetery in Restland, right next door to Burbank Airport. It's a twenty-one-minute drive from Altadena. My family hadn't talked much about Lee after he died, but I found myself grieving his death. Who was Milton Lee Ratcliff? I wanted to know his story.

After thirty-four years, I needed to talk to him. I placed a dozen white roses at his gravesite. It hurt that no one cared enough to get him a headstone. Did anybody care about my daddy? I vowed that I would one day make sure he had a headstone.

My heart was broken, causing panic attacks, when Grandma Jean wouldn't speak to me. She passed away New Year's Eve of 2013. While the first openly gay NFL draft prospect Michael Sam was jockeying for a team I reconnected with my aunt. I now had a perfect picture of my father. Mom never painted one of him.

My Aunty said:

"Your dad was a good person. I remember my mother would do so many things for him. Lee had many friends. His character was a quiet person, not loud or rowdy, and very intelligent. I admired his beautiful handwriting. His hands were long and his white teeth stood out. Lee's hair is what most African

Americans would call 'good hair'. Well groomed always and very neat. He was a handsome man; the ladies loved him. Your dad worked in radio and did extra work on the 'Buddy Holly Story' and a war film."

Dad would tell my aunt how beautiful mom was and how much he loved her. He said he wished he had not cheated and was sorry that he'd made a mistake. He wished he could erase the past and start over again.

She said, "After your father would visit with you and your siblings he would leave and come back drunk, he couldn't deal with the loss of his children, but it was too late—the marriage was over."

Just like dad, very coordinated, quiet, and gifted. I had his all his features, attracting both men and women. The desire to work in the entertainment industry manifested in my teens. I shot my first TV commercial at age sixteen for Chuck E. Cheese, and was eligible to join the Screen Actors Guild.

Thirty-six years later I was reacquainted with my paternal side. My deceased grandfather Milton Ratcliff Sr. served in World War II and great-grandfather Harvey Chaney in WW I. I was very proud to know that I had grandfathers who served the United States of America.

This June 2014, I receive my first literary award from the Bronx Council on the Arts. I will dedicate it to Mr. Milton Lee Ratcliff in remembrance of him for Father's Day.

Bronx Memories

Susan Rotgard

We were so lucky to be accepted for an apartment in the newly built Marble Hill Houses, on 225th Street and Broadway, in 1951. I was nine years old and my brother, Paul, was two. We had always lived downtown and knew nothing of the Bronx.

Marble Hill Houses consisted of eleven buildings, organized around the circumference of a very large circle of grass and trees, except for two buildings, which were across Broadway, on the other side, at 228 Street. Beautiful trees were planted throughout the complex. Some of them were Magnolia trees that blossomed each spring; some were white, some were pink. They are still there and they still blossom.

We lived on the 14th floor in apartment 14K in the second building in from Broadway on 225th street. This apartment had so many windows, with so much light! We looked out at a vast expanse. We could see other parts of the Bronx, the bridge over Spuyten Duyvil. The river. Everything to the south. A lot to the east and west. There were no buildings to obstruct this marvelous view. Our new home felt so open! There were two bedrooms, a living room, bathroom, a kitchen, and dining area at the end of it.

There is a Bronx-born artist, Daniel Hauben, who paints various parts of the Bronx and different scenes from this diverse borough. Some of his paintings are of views which I saw daily from the windows of apartment 14K. When I first saw his work, I recognized so many of his "subjects." He captured them perfectly with his paintbrush. They were a familiar part of my growing up.

We residents of Marble Hill Houses were black, white, Latino/a, Asian, and "other." Everyone pretty much got along. We interacted with each other. Children played together, grew up together. Parents talked to one another. The atmosphere was friendly, which seemed perfectly natural.

I attended the local public elementary school, P.S. 7, on Kingsbridge Avenue near west 231st Street. It was there that I became class conscious. Until then, I had always assumed that everyone's mother worked. Mine did, and not because she had a career or was bored at home, but because she had to, in order for us to live. My stepfather's salary alone was not enough to sustain our family.

When I went to my classmate Karen's home in Riverdale, their apartment had wall-to-wall carpeting. Her father was a lawyer. Her mother did not work, nor did she clean their apartment. They employed a maid. Karen's mother's daily activities consisted mostly of shopping at Alexander's on Fordham Road, for outfits for her daughter. So different from my home, such a different lifestyle, one that I had no idea existed.

In those days, after school I had to get on the #1 train (can't remember if it was called that then) at 231street and Broadway and go to Dyckman Street to pick up my baby brother from nursery school, all the way at the end of the Dyckman Street projects, near the Harlem River Drive. Then back home we went.

This must have been a long trip: the subway and then a very long walk, then the same in reverse. I had to take care of Paul and do a number of chores before either my mother or stepfather came home from work. The good thing about this was that no adults were home in my apartment and friends could come over and we could hang out without parental supervision.

We all liked that.

The Apple Bank on West 231st Street between Corlear and Kingsbridge Avenues (now a computer repair shop) was where I had my first bank account, with my very own passbook. A fun family trip, via the bus that is now the BX9, was to go to Addie Valens Ice Cream Parlor on the Grand Concourse near the Lowe's Paradise. We all pigged out on sundaes there. My stepfather especially enjoyed this, particularly the chocolate fudge sundae. I don't believe this popular ice cream parlor still exists.

About twenty years ago, when my cousin Marcey was visiting us from Mexico, (where she had been living for decades), we took her on a tour of places she had lived in in the Bronx, where she had been born and raised. The Bronx Zoo and Bronx Park had been her childhood playgrounds. Many of the places were gone and/or not at all as she remembered them.

Many years later, when the South Bronx was decimated by landlord neglect, poverty, squalor, and all its concomitant problems, there was a People's Convention organized in a huge empty space in the South Bronx. This was in

1980, when landlords had painted the windows of all the abandoned buildings, of which there were many, with curtains and some plants on the windowsills, as if the apartments were occupied. There was row upon row, empty building after empty building, and street after street of this bizarre sight.

This was after the 1960s, when there was a lot of political organizing going on. People all over the country and here in New York City were coming together, to protest the war in Vietnam, demanding civil rights, better housing, access to health care and education. The Black Power movement, the women's movement, the Puerto Rican movement, the beginning of the lesbian and gay movement, were all emerging. Change was in the air. Grassroots organizing rose.

I was sixteen when I left home, never to return. That's a story in itself, as is everything that followed. I felt as if I'd escaped. Our outwardly bright, open home contained an extremely dysfunctional, sad and unhappy family. I could not wait to get out and so I made it happen.

All things change. It is a law of nature. The Bronx is not exempt from this and it, too, has changed over the years. And I, who have also changed so much over the decades since I left, have returned to the Bronx these many years later, and once again call the Bronx home.

Theresa

Michael Cruz

Every morning she sat at the same table in Burger King—by the window. There, she repeated her life story to whoever was within earshot.

She was sixty-five years old. She had an aneurism and a son and a grandson, the latter of questionable lineage, but rarely saw either. Her husband left her for another woman. She raised two foster daughters. In family court with one to sever ties that never should've been tied in the first place.

Aside from sneakers that were once white and ill-fitting jeans, she wore red. A three-quarter length coat. A floral hat. A knit sweater that did little to conceal cleavage gone south of the border.

After breakfast, she put an unlit cigarette to her lips. Steadying her cane, she acted as if she had places to go and people to see. Home to the solitude of a one-bedroom apartment. Early evening, before the credits rolled on her favorite television game show "Jeopardy", her bifocal eyes grew weary and gave way to sleep.

Enabling her to step out of the present and into the past.

When the Bronx Was Burning

Lucy Aponte

Wednesday, October 15, 1975.

Two years before sportscaster Howard Cosell coined the phrase, "The Bronx is burning," my baby lay peaceful in her bassinet. Daylight shone through my bedroom window on that blistery, fall day. The smell of smoke came into the apartment, as my older children got ready for school. In the last few months, I had smelled smoke three times, checked, but found nothing.

Recent break-ins in the building caused me to nail my bedroom window shut. Opening the door, I checked the hall, again finding nothing. I had practiced fire drills with my children, having experienced fire as a teenager. Hugging and kissing my kids, I sent them off to school with my neighbor. I was still recovering from giving birth two weeks before. Going down six flights and walking back up a steep hill, with a newborn was too much, yet.

I loved our apartment. Each morning the sun lit up the bedrooms, while the moonlight through the living room window offered a breathtaking view of the Harlem River at night. In my nightgown and shoeless, I moved the bassinet into the living room, ready for my cup of coffee. I indulged myself in the intoxicating scent of a newborn, with a kiss on my baby's cheek, and felt I was in Heaven.

The smell of smoke came in again. I checked the kitchen. Nothing was burning. As I reached to turn the apartment doorknob, something told me, to touch the door. It was hot! FIRE!

My brain reeled: "Don't open the door."

Whirling around, I ran for the baby. BOOM!

A thick, black cloud enveloped me, filling the foyer, obliterating the light and everything in sight—behind, around, and in front of me. I was in total blackness. My senses went dull: I couldn't see, hear, smell, or feel. My sense of direction was gone.

"Oh, God, the baby. Where is she?"

I fought the panic.

"Calm down," I told myself. "Find the baby and get out! Feel for the bassinet. Keep moving forward. Careful. Was it still standing, or was it blown down? Feel with your feet. Feel with your hands."

Sweeping my hands across the blackened, choking air for the bassinet and feeling the floor with my feet for the baby, I found it was still standing! My hands reached inside. But I couldn't tell if I was touching my baby or a stuffed toy.

I remembered I had a blanket over her. Wrapping everything on the mattress into the blanket, I pressed the precious bundle tight to my chest, protecting her from the smoke.

"Please lead me to the fire escape," I said.

With determination, I found my bed. Pressing against the edge to guide me towards the headboard, I felt the crib to my left and the window in front of me—which led to the fire escape. I yanked the window and felt resistance. I tried again. It wouldn't budge.

Horrified, I felt the nails that held the window shut. Placing the bundle on the bed, I secured another blanket tight to keep the smoke away. I began my mantra, "Don't forget the baby, don't forget the baby."

As a teen, I often babysat for my neighbors. In a fire, they forgot their baby. He was found dead in his carriage. I swore then, I would not forget mine, if I were ever in a fire.

Determined to survive, I wrapped a sheet around my arm. I smashed the window. Glass broke. A suffocating draft rushed past my head and through the broken window. I stuck my head out, gasping for air.

But the thick smoke kept me from taking a clear breath and I couldn't see out. Grabbing the baby, I pushed through the glass. I feared we'd die there, or blinded by the smoke, we'd fall to our deaths from the fire escape.

Suddenly, hands were grabbing and pulling me, but I couldn't see who was doing this. I felt myself being pulled out, as I desperately clung to my baby, trying to keep the glass from cutting her.

"Give me the baby!" said a young firefighter.

I couldn't let her go.

"Give me the baby!" he said. "Go down backwards."

I handed the baby over. The covers came loose, as he threw the bundle with my tiny baby over his right shoulder. The cover hung at his knees. I feared the baby could slip over his shoulder, or from below to the ground.

"It's a tiny baby," I said, barely audible.

I was terrified he might think the long blanket held a toddler, rather than a tiny newborn. I kept putting one hand up, ready to catch her, should she slip out. My heart was in my throat, as I descended, backwards, the wind, threatening to blow me off.

At two steps above the sidewalk I jumped down, desperate to have my baby safe in my arms. Grabbing her as he stepped down, I pummeled his chest with my fist.

"It's a tiny baby, it's a tiny baby!" I cried, holding her tight.

The firefighter said nothing. But the look in his eyes was one of understanding, as he steered us towards the ambulance. This man had gone to rescue us, when a neighbor yelled, pointing up, "There's a woman up there, with a baby!"

To this day I am grateful to him and that neighbor for saving us.

Firefighters from the Bronx, Manhattan, and New Jersey battled that three-hour five-alarm fire. My next door neighbor nearly died with her bedridden husband, before they were brought down in a cherry-picker.

The young couple across the hall lost their dogs, who in desperation to escape, plunged six stories to their deaths. Terrified babies and children shivered in diapers and pajamas. My kids and I lost our beautiful home and all our possessions that day.

When the Bronx was burning.

I Saw Fordham Road

Louie Santiago

"Next stop Yankee Stadium," the train conductor announced.

My heart skipped a beat as I put down the Archie comic book I was reading. Yankee Stadium, I repeated to myself. Can't be. The next stop is 149th Street and 3rd Avenue. I started to panic.

It was May, 1966. I was eleven years old; short for my age and riding the subway alone. This was about the fourth time I had been allowed to take the train on my own, and it could have turned out to be my last solo trip.

For over a month now, I had been visiting my grandmother alone. I was a big boy, hot stuff. Traveling all the way to Brooklyn from The Bronx and back. It was a long trip too, a little over an hour. I was the happiest kid in the world. I didn't know any other kid my age that was allowed to make this journey on their own.

"Next stop Chambers Street," the conductor announced.

Another successful trip I thought, although I still had more than half the trip ahead of me. I got off and climbed the long staircase which would lead me to the #5 train. I heard a train approaching and started to run, reaching the platform as the doors opened and jumped in. I patted myself on the back.

At the next two stops, I checked to make sure that I was heading in the right direction. The next time I looked up I saw 149th Street and Grand Concourse. Great, I thought.

I was overconfident until I heard the announcement for Yankee Stadium. I kept thinking that the next stop was supposed to be 149th Street and 3rd Avenue. I panicked and heard my heart beating over the rattling noise of the train. What to do? Light started flowing into the car. This cannot be happening. It was one stop too soon. The train should still be underground.

I was lost!

I leaned against the train door and stared outside, in disbelief. My stomach rumbled. The scenery I looked at did not look familiar at all. Where was I? I saw a big baseball park as I had heard Yankee Stadium announced again. I knew it was in The Bronx, but not in my neighborhood.

I looked around with big bulging eyes and spotted the #4 on the window, where #5 should have been. My mind refused to register the #4, and then it clicked. I had jumped into the train at Brooklyn Bridge without making sure it was the #5. My father must have drilled this into me a thousand times, while I replied, "I know, I know."

I could stop a policeman or look at the map. *Relax.* I tried to control myself as I walked over to the map on wobbly legs. I felt like crying but controlled myself and tried to remember what my father showed me. I found where I was supposed to be on the #5 and where I was on the #4. I felt better because they didn't look so far away from each other on the map.

Then my prayer was answered.

I saw Fordham Road!

I wanted to jump up and down while I kept my finger on Fordham Road. It was the only stop I recognized along the 4 line. Never mind that I wasn't sure where I was, but I'd been at Fordham Road before. Back then I didn't know the difference between east, west, north or south and it did not matter—I would get off.

I looked over the railing as the train pulled away. Construction on Co-op City was just beginning, on what had once been the Freedomland amusement park. Before that it was swampland. The flight to Co-op would not begin for another two years, so the neighborhood was still predominately Jewish, Italian, and Irish American.

As I gazed over the crowd below me, I looked up and noticed the first of many landmarks that would take me home. It was the ten-story clock tower with four faces, each now frozen at different times of the day, the building vacant. It once housed the executive offices of The Dollar Savings Bank. I wasn't sure, but I believed it was near a big street.

I exited the train station and was lucky because it led me east, in the direction that I needed to go. I walked unsure, heading toward the clock tower and the big street. After a couple of blocks, I stumbled into another landmark, Alexander's department store, now another part of the Bronx's past. I saw the clock tower and the big street, the famous Grand Concourse. I knew that I was on the right track.

I walked down Fordham Road and saw (to my delight) the elevated train that I was familiar with—the 3rd Avenue El, which would stop running in another six years. I picked up my pace and saw the Sears department store, which I often passed with my mother on our way home. Years later, it turned into a fraction of its size, selling only appliances.

I still wasn't quite sure how to get home, but I kept running into familiar landmarks which gave me hope. I saw the big school, Fordham University. Across the street I saw Theodore Roosevelt High School, which two of my sisters would later attend.

I kept walking faster, now led by my instinct. Two more landmarks convinced me that I was definitely heading in the right direction. The first was Fordham Hospital, now closed and torn down, and the second was a street named Crotona Avenue. I knew the elementary school I had attended, P.S. 92, was on this avenue.

I turned right because I thought I remembered it was the way the bus turned, not knowing for sure. I made it home that day, very tired, hungry, and extremely proud of myself.

I never told anyone this story before for fear that my privilege would have been taken away and I would not have been able to visit my grandmother on my own again. I was lost and found my way because I saw Fordham Road.

Eighties Bronx as Seen Through the Eyes of an Eight-Year-Old

Yadhira Gonzalez-Taylor, Esq.

I carry the legacy of a bifurcated childhood. This can be both a blessing and a curse. For years I lived in the tropics and my backyard was made up of mountaintops, magical places in the eyes of a little child. The other part of that childhood was spent in the Bronx where I had dilapidated buildings for a view.

Overnight, and without my consent, I was removed from a luscious green world and dumped on the cold, damp streets of the Bronx. Where I once walked barefoot, on red cool clay, I now wore shoes to avoid getting cut by glass or pricked by an addict's needle.

Although I was born in the Bronx, I left for Puerto Rico at four and returned with my mother when I was eight. My mother and I came to the Bronx, in search of doctors for my brother, a chronic asthmatic since birth.

New York City meant medicine that was not available on the island. This, my native city was not welcoming. The language I never learned seemed cold, coarse, unnatural, and offensive. Los gringos sounded like they were barking at me. I missed the minimization and comfort of Puerto Rican slang.

I understood nothing and resorted to invented sign language to survive. The cold and wind felt like paper cuts on my exposed skin. At my age I wasn't supposed to know what an addict was. I wasn't supposed to wonder why there was war-like rubble everywhere. Instead, I should have been swinging in hammocks and eating bacalao and cassava.

I wondered what happened to the trees. They all seemed to be sparsely corralled throughout playgrounds made of plastic and metal where little needles littered the landings of the slides. My new world had real life rubber puppets. They were alive, and in a precocious flaccid manner they could touch the ground and spring back, eyes still slanted, sleepy—oblivious to the pain that delivered them into such a state.

In my new world burning mattresses flew out of fifth-story windows, pushed out by towering Irish firemen, with funny mustaches and dark coats, like knights, saving us from our plight. But even then, in our urban blight, the neighbors were decent and they looked out for us kids.

Crack had other plans.

Crack came at the pinnacle of the arson age and it was the final blow to the Bronx. Like a beaten down drunk, punched right in the face with the huge fist of a bully, the remaining hold of my future beloved was lost. "Crack heads" were a different breed of addict. The rubbery puppet dope heads, didn't bother anyone. They were in their own world.

The crack heads were agitated, aggressive, and willing to do whatever it took to get high. Now I had to watch out for the skinny, disheveled, excited people. My mom would say: "They might try to rob you for a fix."

In my paranoia I looked out for stalkers, slashers, flashers, druggies, prostitutes and pimps, because they could jump out of dark alleys and snatch me up in a split second. Crack made the sidewalks crunchy and I made a game of stepping on the tiny plastic vials crushing them under my Burnside Avenue-bought Chinese shoes.

With little to do, I watched people for entertainment. I watched the fake blond picking vials from her crotch to hand to her customers. I watched the man on 181st Street and Grand Avenue yelling "la jara" or "agua"—a word uttered by lookouts signaling the appearance of police on the block.

I watched my first crush, flirting with other girls who were allowed to roam free on the block when I wasn't—all hope of love lost. I watched my father, standing on the corner, beer in hand, an angry gleam in his eye, a sure sign that we would be running that night.

I watched the prostitute servicing the john on a dirty mattress in the rubble behind my building. Other times, I watched her arguing with the johns who shortchanged her over something she called blowjobs.

I no longer lived in a world of green, sunshine, and homemade piraguas. Now I existed in a box made of cement. For me, education, and social stratification were the ticket out. For my sad world, the golden ticket was gentrification and affordable housing programs.

The grit of the Bronx diminished, annihilating the squeegee man, and most homelessness. I still live here but on the other side of the Bronx, the part that didn't burn down in the time of my childhood. I live in the Bronx that my eight-year-old eyes never saw, the side only available for purchase.

My beloved Boogie Down, with all its current problems, is better now than it was then. Thirty-three years later, it is much better than it was when I first landed here.

Sometimes people assume that I went to private school when they hear I grew up to become an attorney. They assume that this would've been the only way for anyone to have survived, thrived, succeeded and escaped from the trash they mistakenly imagine my childhood to have been.

I explain that I went to the public elementary schools lining the aqueduct. That I thank the people who pushed and supported me, even the ones who discouraged me. I explain to them that I did, for a part of my formative years, live in a crazy little spot in the world, located on four corners in the middle of shit, filth, and scum.

I admit to them that I am a person who lived in constant dysfunction, inside and outside the home. Yet despite the odds, I survived with less just like they did with more, a concept difficult to understand for most.

El Misinformed

Marte-Bautista

A library can wield misinformation and danger. I found both in one of them. As I ate a peanut butter sandwich underneath the stairway's 'don't eat, don't drink' sign, this Greek-American yelled into his cell phone. His green eyes turned to me for a chat.

How was I to know that I was inviting into my life one who would upset my social life? Who had me starring in my own 'survival of the fittest' episode?

I let this guy stay with me at my place, for his Brazilian wife and he were killing each other. Not that he could leave her, for she was capable of sexual positions he never thought possible. Some tourist friends warned me about him. My friends' animosity came from hearing their nationality and color identities stripped from them as he spoke.

"Are Brazilians Hispanic or Latin?" homeboy asked, after complaining of whites tourists changing the Afro-Caribbean nature of countries like the Dominica Republic, Venezuela, and Brazil.

"The Spanish conquerors were and are whites and there is no color called by the name of a language on Planet Earth," the indigenous, black, and Caucasian Latin-American tourists shouted in unison.

I had to tell them that it wasn't this guy's fault that a 1970 census, the media and interest groups, made this labeling a requirement for us to apply and qualify for anything.

I was even flattered with his insistence to see me as a New York Rican, my clear foreigner traits notwithstanding. Homeboy was excited with me and would mimic everything I did.

The lesbians from the apartment next door said they believed that homeboy was "in the closet and has a crush on you." After they broke down what "in the closet" meant, I voiced my doubt. They made a bet with me.

One day, with the lesbians hiding in the closet (no pun intended), I had this punk dress up with me, in Brazilian flag speedos for Ju-jitsu that my wife had sent me and to wrest in. I blew the fumes of a make-believe magic hot tea into his mouth, which ended in a casual kiss. I looked down to his crotch; though his seemed bigger than mine he barely got aroused.

I called out the neighbors and stuffed my twenty dollars in my speedos, for he was no gay.

The illegal immigrant-chick probably fearing I could mess up her plans of getting the green card, plus having a full time sex-slave, went on attack mode. She got into homeboy's head that we were doing shit behind his back. He came back, and after a loud argument, he disappeared from my life.

He contacted me a couple of years afterward, asking to see me. Problem is, when I see danger I don't run away from it—I let it get to me "The rappers-thugs should worry almost no one," I would explain to clean-cut professionals in my favorite Albanian lounge on Arthur Avenue.

I would argue that it was the nerdy-looking folks, who tend to be potential psychos, whom we should watch out for. Well, I should have practiced my own advice when I let this creature into my place to spend the night.

When I got up from my bed, where I sleep naked, he was standing around stabbing himself with a toy arrowhead until I could see red dots. I grew up with Ascetic Catholics putting pain on themselves to discipline the flesh—do you think Mr. Eminem here was going to impress me?

I saw his eyes change…using the typical psycho intimidation techniques he expected to make me run in fear!

What did I do instead?

I stood up into an elegant pose, took an empty bottle, uncapped it, and urinated inside. This enraged him enough to prevent him from acting in cold blood, like a good psycho. Turning red he completely lost control and jumped on me, with one hand grabbing the bottle.

Like a good Third World man, I swung back and forth the contents of the bottle splashing over his straight hair. His hands went around my neck, and I kept swinging using my body weight to drag him over to the kitchen, screaming, "That's all you can do?" through his choking grip.

I reached for the doorknob and everything went dark.

When my vision cleared up again I was on the house porch, a bucket in my hand, looking sideways to an astonished neighbor two houses to my left. I looked toward the house's door glass panel and saw the wacko's impassive face peering out.

Survival instinct made me shout for him that the cops would be dropping in any time. He burst out of the door; passing by me, and like Frankenstein was gone. The cops came of course when all the fun was over. The ambulance came for me, and took me to the hospital.

After a few hours I left the hospital. I let go of the haunting memories from my moments of near death. "But where am I?" my inquiring eyes asked in silence. I fell into a walking rhythm while stretching my neck and arms, taking in my environment.

There are Mexican indigenous, Albanian, Slavic, and Dominican women pushing baby strollers while shopping. I kept finding black American teen and adults standing around corners eyeing with curiosity as Dominican guys flirted with girls passing by, while making fun of each other one minute and embracing the next in the male bonding that some local guys feel insecure to display.

I see throngs of students spilling out of Fordham University, walking in all directions. I hear and brush past a rich mix of cultures. I keep on walking. Wherever these throngs are going I find my feet going—for I am tired of running alone.

The Kelly Street I Knew

Sonia Fuentes Resto

The deafening roar of the IRT elevated train as it entered the Intervale Avenue Station rested for a brief moment before introducing the quieter sound of the subway doors opening, then quickly closing. On weekdays, these sounds were repeated every half hour.

At the age of six I was accustomed to the rumble of the trains from the proximity of our fourth floor window. I enjoyed watching the riders entering or exiting the cars, always in a rush.

I often wondered, "Why are they running? Where are they going?"

On special occasions, my parents would take me up those steep train station stairs to ride the magnificent iron monster for a ride "downtown."

Oh, what a treat that was! Going to see the skyscrapers or Radio City Music Hall in Manhattan was an event that made an everlasting impression on me.

Living on Kelly Street in the Bronx during the early 1950s was very convenient for my family. Titi Anita, my aunt, lived on the next block over, on a magically curved street known as "Banana Kelly".

Tío Pepe lived on Simpson Street and Titi Tona lived on Prospect Avenue, both just a subway stop away. On the corner of Kelly Street and Westchester Avenue, just a few steps from our building, were the local friendly farmacia, bodega, and the family doctor's office.

On that same avenue was el vivero, the live poultry slaughterhouse I dreaded visiting. The acrid smell of wet feathers and the helpless squawking of the fowl as they were held against the large shaving machines were overwhelming for the animal lover in me. I was never able to witness the actual slaughtering process, since I feigned illness whenever my abuela encouraged me to watch.

She thought my behavior was childish because she slaughtered chickens often as a young girl. The workers at the poultry place recognized my terror and always offered a balloon as consolation. To this day, I associate balloons with the butchering of chickens. However, once the fowl was in a pot with Puerto Rican spices and herbs like adobo, cilantro, and fresh garlic, and stewed to perfection at home, I delighted in savoring my favorite pieces.

My family lived at 971 Kelly Street when I was born in 1951. The beige limestone four-story building had twenty apartments. We lived in 1D, a two-bedroom apartment for my parents, grandmother, two brothers, my baby sister and me.

My parents were close friends with the families that lived in apartments 2D, 3D, 1C, and 4E. All other neighbors in that building were known to us by name. Most of them had extended families living with them or close by. There were few single parent families, and everyone seemed to have a job.

The hallways, front stoops, and back stairs were always immaculate and people never loitered. I cannot remember a time when any of the residents of the other small buildings on Kelly Street "hung out" in the front stoops for extended periods of time. Everyone remained indoors for the most part, even during the sweltering heat of New York summers.

My mother was a beautician and made house calls whenever she wasn't working at her own salon. One of her favorite clients lived two buildings away from us on the fifth floor. In order to avoid going down four flights of stairs and then climbing another five flights to service her friend, my mother had a special plan.

She would take my sister and I with her when she went up to the roof of our building. She would jump across the adjacent roof edges to the adjoining building, extending her protective arms for us to do the same. There was such tranquility and silence up there. The tar was always soft and smelled like a brand new doll.

I recall my excitement of being up so high and able to see Kelly Street below, which seemed miles away. I was always excited about these adventures, because to a seven-year-old, it felt like flying.

On Saturday mornings my father washed and waxed the linoleum floors in our apartment. The smell of King Pine gave us a sense of renewal and cleanliness. At the same time the Victrola played Mantovani's *The Soul of Spain* at full volume.

I would shadow dance to the toreador's entrance music to the bullfighter's arena. By the afternoon hours, my father was dressed to the nines with his suit, tie and fedora hat. Most men wore felt fedoras every day even with casual clothes. In the winter they wore long coats and white silk scarves in the style of Argentinian tango sensation, Carlos Gardel.

For special occasions, women always wore dresses, stockings and high heels. Fancy hairstyles, long necklaces, and dark red lipstick were a must. Every family picture I have from that era is testimony to this fact. No Puerto Rican woman ever dared to wear slacks during those years.

Saturday nights were times of celebration. On special Saturday afternoons, my sister and I were dressed in beautiful "can-can" party dresses and shiny patent leather shoes. The parties were always adult centered, even if it was a child's birthday, baptism, first communion or graduation.

My father would jokingly say, "We even celebrated the baptism of a doll."

The kids were usually sent to play in the bedrooms. The coats were piled high on the beds creating a distinct mixture of Chanel #5 and Varon Dandy aftershave floating in the air. It was a wonderful delight as a child to fall asleep under all those coats. I remember feeling so warm and protected brushing against the fake furs.

I can still hear the slow-moving bolero, "Bésame Mucho", and laughter from what seemed far, far away.

Television family nights were very predictable.

On Saturday nights, my parents, abuela, Titi Anita and Tío Hernández would rush through dinner in order to watch *The Lawrence Welk Show*. I relished being bilingual and bicultural and I was so proud of the fact that my family felt the same way.

In a way, it was like living in two worlds. The elders also enjoyed *The Ed Sullivan Show* and *The Wonderful World of Disney* on Sundays. We spoke only Spanish at home but learning English was paramount. The music we listened to on the radio and record player was in Spanish.

My teenaged brothers preferred Frank Sinatra and *American Bandstand* but they also listened to one of the most popular music of the fifties; the mambo. I first heard Tito Puente, Tito Rodríguez and Machito—the Big Three from the Palladium Ballroom in that Kelly Street living room.

Although the media image of the South Bronx has been portrayed as a dangerous and impoverished, I remember it as a safe and nurturing environment. Our family life was simple and very enjoyable.

The 1950s was a very innocent and family-oriented decade for many of us. Before falling asleep, the last sound I heard was the familiar roar of the train. I could count on its scheduled arrival and departure. It never changed, just like my memories of Kelly Street.

Bill's in Calvary

Toby Z. Liederman

Tom sent an email yesterday saying that Bill was in Calvary. My heart dropped. He'd been suffering from serious emphysema for such a long time that maybe his lungs had had enough. At Calvary Hospital, in the Morris Park section of the Bronx, he'd be nurtured by skilled professionals who'd either find solutions to help him live, or his days would be pain-free and serene.

After hearing the news, I began thinking of how our friendship had grown. It was through good ole' Bronx Volunteerism.

Flashback: 2010, early spring.

What made me even think of planning a birthday lunch for her? Well, I live on City Island, surrounded by breathtaking Pelham Bay Park, happy at having discovered how my Massachusetts roots connect me to this place in surprising ways. It has a New England fault-line, reminds me of Cape Cod (I call it "My Seedy Cape Cod").

She also came from Massachusetts (in the 1600s!) and ended up living very close by. I remember seeing her statue on the State House lawn in Boston, but I didn't know much more about her until about ten years ago, when a friend and I cofounded Hutchinson River Restoration Project. I became totally consumed by her and her river.

When women were expected to be silent, to obey without thinking, she spoke up for what she believed, in spite of harsh consequences from church-state authoritarian rulers. Anne Marbury Hutchinson was an early American hero, and I wanted more people to know about her. As I discovered later, so did Bill.

Enthused by her courage and strength, I thought, why not celebrate her?

I sent a gazillion invitations for a lunch party to commemorate her 419th birthday anniversary at Split Rock/Pelham Bay Golf Course Café on Shore Road, July 21st, 2010, her likely birthdate.

Five City Island friends showed up, plus Carol Twomey, and her husband Bill. Bill was the President of the East Bronx History Forum and Bronx history writer for *The Bronx Times*.

I was thrilled they were there!

And what did Bill do as we were ending our meal? He stood up and said what a great idea it was and how important it was to remember and honor this woman who virtually helped mold America's early history, who lived right here in the Bronx, yet was so little known!

He encouraged us to gather every year to be sure she wasn't forgotten. Here was another person counting her as one of America's earliest feminists!

Among the earliest Puritan settlers, Anne lived in Massachusetts in the 1630s, until she was banished and excommunicated from Boston, first travelling—pregnant and by foot—with some of her family and a small contingent of followers to Rhode Island, where Roger Williams and his group welcomed them, all eager to experience freedom of religion and separation of church and state.

In 1642, probably August, she and a party of sixteen, six of her children, plus some relatives and servants, came to what is now the Bronx, likely near today's Co-Op City—what was then forests, marshland, swamps and brooks. It was land inhabited for centuries by tribespeople we call Native Americans.

Here she came, settling near the river that would be named for her, on land that early maps show as Hutchinson's Meadow, Hutchinson's Field, and Hutchinson's Land.

She was likely in the wrong place at the wrong time, killed in 1643 in what was probably retaliation by the natives for a horrendous massacre by the Dutch. Her impact lives on, not only locally, but nationally, though not enough even know it.

Separation of church and state, freedom of speech, and the right to freely assemble are all part of our Bill of Rights. "Thank you, Anne, dear foremother. You paved the way."

Bill's words at the luncheon sparked my enthusiasm. On February 4, 2011, Pelham Bay Park Administrator Marianne Anderson, Alfredo Perez, Park Program Director, and I met with about nineteen people at Huntington Free Library in Westchester Square for our fledgling brainstorming meeting.

"The Anne Hutchinson Year", celebrating the anniversary of her 420th birthday, was born.

During 2011, organizations and individuals throughout the Bronx and Westchester responded far beyond imagination! When two Anne Hutchinson Schools, one in the Bronx and one in Eastchester, created absolutely fantastic assemblies, exhibitions and projects about Anne and her legacy, my friend and coworker Violet said to me:

"Toby, if we do nothing else the whole year, we've succeeded."

She was right. Nothing could top what those kids and teachers produced, the fact that so many children now knew about our heroic foremother.

Not that Bill and I were in touch often, mind you. He was simply 'there', like when a few organizations backed off, or when volunteers didn't come through. Sometimes he was the only community leader to show any interest. He republished his earlier biography of Anne in *The Bronx Times*. Sometimes he would simply say how happy he was with the project.

His luncheon urgings came true big time! My committee and I hosted close to forty events! We even planted a Roxbury Russet apple tree in her honor, which you can see free of charge on the grounds of Bartow Pell Mansion and Museum on Shore Road.

Yes, it was a wondrous year.

Bill resigned as president during the year because of his health, but we still kept in touch. Happily, he was well enough to co-host our 2012 birthday luncheon on City Island, but in 2013, when we combined with HRRP on a Hutchinson River cleanup and picnic, it was without Bill.

Now he was in Calvary. And who knew? Even as I completed this memoir, he improved daily! He would hopefully be well enough to inaugurate her 425th, coming up in 2016…

I've already got the title: "The Anne Hutchinson Year 2016: Dedicated to Bill Twomey, Founder and First President of the East Bronx History Forum, Historian, Friend."

Wake Me Up at 6:30

Shavonne Bell

"Wake me up at 6:30," she said.

I contorted my face with confusion. On most days, she didn't roll out of bed before noon—and that was on a lucky day.

Her gold earrings reflected the light from the chandelier hanging above the octagon-shaped glass table in the foyer. I stared at the slightly crooked picture frame that held her bachelor's degree in Computer Science and Engineering from Massachusetts Institute of Technology. Everyone always said she was "too smart for her own good," but I often looked at that degree, wondering what I would make of myself in the future.

She said goodnight and made her way to the only bedroom in our tiny apartment in the Bronx.

"Goodbye!" I yelled as I focused my attention back to the television in the living room.

I laughed to myself. She hated when I said "goodbye" instead of "goodnight" because "goodbye" felt like forever, but I had already developed a habit of doing things just to annoy her.

As a child, I suffered from frequent nightmares and every night without fail, I slept with her in her bed. So, it was particularly strange when I found myself yawning and lying down on the navy blue leather couch, alone. Since she went to bed before I did, I imagined that she waited for me to come crawling under her blanket, like I usually did, before dozing off.

I jolted awake and groaned when the alarm clock on my cell phone sang my favorite Beethoven song at 5 a.m. Rubbing the sleepiness out of my eyes, I made my way to her bedroom and peeked in. Her nightgown had shifted off her left shoulder, but she was still sleeping peacefully.

I quietly crept inside and sat down at the computer. My high school graduation was approaching faster than I had anticipated, and I had to put together a last-minute valedictorian speech that I wasn't prepared to give. By the time I finished typing it up, it was nearly 6:30 a.m.

"Wake up!" I called out.

I sucked my teeth. I knew waking her up was not going to be an easy task. Everyone knew it was impossible to get her out of bed without a fight and we played that game every morning. Trampling the junk she had sprawled out on the floor, I yelled again, but to no avail.

I touched her face, but my fingertips could not recognize the coldness on her body. Her hazel-colored contacts stared right into my natural brown eyes as I slapped her face continuously, until my hand grew numb.

No reaction.

I lifted her stiff arm, only to have it drop back down with an amplified thud onto the soft mattress she lay on. Unable to admit that she had already turned blue, I stumbled towards the phone as the world stopped spinning and everything around me felt like a trance.

From the fourth floor of my building, I could hear the ambulance make its way across Fordham Road and up Andrews Avenue. The sirens played over and over like a broken record. I opened the apartment door for the three strangers who dashed to her room.

It would have been an appropriate time to yell and cry and beg for answers, but instead I found myself staring in her full-length mirror, wondering if I would be late for school again. Minutes, or maybe merely seconds, passed by before one of the paramedics told me there was nothing they could do.

"Your mother's been dead all night," he said.

His words were a sharp knife to my heart, cutting me deep with no remorse. I tried to process what was going on, but nothing made sense in my head until I shifted my attention to the small aluminum foil ball of cocaine wrapped up next to her nightstand. Although the coroners would later announce the cause of death as heart disease, I knew better.

I studied her lifeless body atop the gold sheets that tightly hugged her queen-sized mattress. The knot in my throat grew bigger and it took every ounce of courage I had to turn away. As I left her room, I silently scolded myself for not sleeping in her bed for the first time, but it didn't seem to matter anyway. I whispered the softest "goodbye" and was certain, this time, she knew I wasn't saying it just to annoy her.

Joe and Jose – by Olga Kitt

Snow and Fog

B. Lynn Carter

It's probably because of what happened to Reggie. That's probably why whenever I conjure up memories of my childhood on the block, they never feature snow. My childhood memories are almost never set in the winter. Somehow most memories I have of frolicking in the snow have all been shrouded in fog.

Looking back on those days now, I have to admit that my crowd always did things to the extreme. We got the most out of those whirlwind childhood days, those spring days, those autumn days, but mostly those summer days—the days when your friends were your family and you all functioned as one.

I love the memories of summer, memories of stickball. If you could roof the ball you got to launch your old sneakers up and over the telephone wires, a testament to your status. My sneakers stayed firmly on my feet.

At Orchard Beach we all swam out to the buoys. It was thirty feet of water in high tide. It was simply required. You did it whether or not you could swim. I was not much of a swimmer but despite the admonishments from Chino, the lifeguard, I'd tread water, doggie-paddle along, or turn on my back and float when I was winded.

One way or another I'd make it. I was part of the crowd.

With the autumn came football, two-hand touch, sewer-to-sewer down the middle of the street. Only, we did it on roller-skates. I have to admit that my skating skills were also not quite up to par, but I persevered.

In the spring we flew kites. Only, our kites had double-edged razor blades attached to their tails. They'd fly up over the buildings, up above the rooftops. They'd soar up so far that I was sure they'd scrape the sky. They flew past our boundaries, challenging; taunting, invading the turfs of neighboring blocks. There they did battle in the sky. Zigging and dodging, dipping and slashing, until one of the soaring combatants was cut down, defeated.

The descending kite was the prize to be claimed by the victor. Actually, my mother never let me handle the bladed kites, so I generally cheered from the sidelines.

But the winter days, the days with snow, they are foggy in my mind. And I think, now, it's because of what happened to Reggie.

If I force myself, I can vaguely recall snowball fights and snow drifts that towered over my head. And I do remember the time that the "big kids" picked up a Volkswagen, placed it on the sidewalk, and covered it with snow. We played on that mound of snow for days.

The owner reported it stolen. He didn't discover the truth until the thaw. And now that I'm thinking about it, I recall how we would barrel down the steep Freeman Street hill on makeshift cardboard sleds, nearly mowing down all those unsuspecting subway commuters as they made their way up the hill after work.

These are the easy memories I have of winter and snow. These are the images that I welcome, that I allow to gently emerge from my guarded catalog of precious recollections. But the thing with Reggie was so random and haunting that I had to wrap it in mist, fold it neatly and put it away in the back of my mind. Now it's just lurking there somewhere, like fog.

I didn't witness it firsthand. I wasn't there. Mercifully, all I saw was the frozen scarlet stain left behind on the fresh white snow. And on some ridiculous level it was mesmerizing, the contrast, the pattern, the smooth magenta lines and spikes, like a large red snowflake against the stark white canvas. I recall we all stood staring at it. No one spoke. We just stared until some adult came along and shoveled it up, like a wounded animal, and took it away.

I think now that the retelling of what happened was worse than the actual event. In reality, it must have been fast, uncomplicated, quick . . . and final. Reggie was not doing anything reckless. He wasn't haphazardly treading water in the middle of the ocean.

He wasn't engaging in cutthroat kite games or kamikaze sledding down the Freeman Street hill. He emerged from his house smiling, stood on his front porch, waved at the kids that were romping on the Volkswagen mound, took one step, his last step, slipped and fell, his head hitting the brick staircase, hard, as he descended.

It became the subject of urban legend on my block. Everyone who saw it saw it differently. It grew more gruesome with each retelling. He flew four feet into the air, they said. His head imploded, erupted, they said. Blood spewed from his mouth, his eyes bulged from his head, his arms and legs were bent at impossible angles.

Once planted, these images grew in my mind. For a while they tortured my dreams, before I was able to wrap them in fog and put them away. All I really understood, at the time, was that Reggie was one of us and then he was gone…gone, never to return.

His only legacy, a somber blemish in the snow. The image of his face having long since slipped from memory. And snow never looked the same.

School Days

Barbara Gurkin Fasciani

Whenever I think about P.S. 28, I smell warm crayons. I was filled with that aroma every time I opened the door to my beloved elementary school on Tremont and Anthony Avenues. It was built in the late 1800s and was the school my father attended.

The outdoor yard had two entrances; one on Tremont Avenue and the other around the block on Mount Hope Place. The indoor yard took the place of a gym. The front of the building faced Anthony Avenue.

It was constructed with a façade of tall, Doric columns and three or four long flat steps which ran the length of the building. The formidable entrance was reserved for teachers. It opened to a wide staircase with a polished mahogany banister.

This staircase, which was off-limits to students, was also filled with the heavy odor of a crayon factory. On one very special occasion, I was permitted to enter those hallowed halls through this Parthenonian entrance. It was the day I made my stage debut.

I was almost six years old and would be graduating from kindergarten in a couple of weeks. I loved going to school and I loved my teacher, Miss Greco. Every day for two hours I played and socialized in Room 102. My favorite activity was the pegboard.

I could spend hours fitting those multicolored pegs into the board with so many little holes, creating swirling patterns of color. When I wasn't working with the pegs or the puzzles, I struggled with Ann, the little red-headed girl who lived across the street from me, for the affections of Steven Cohen, a plump boy who wore glasses and a crew-cut.

Ann threw a chair at me once, to dissuade me from my pursuits. But I continued undaunted and always picked Steven when we played Bluebird through My Window. Eventually, we both forgot about Steven, but not about each other. We are still great friends.

In May of 1954, plans for a talent show were announced. I loved to sing and had been told by adoring and polite relatives that I was "very talented" and had "so much personality" (as if an extra dose had been thrown in for good measure). I guess my mother was my biggest fan because she encouraged me to participate in this event.

I selected from my limited repertoire, "When the Red, Red Robin Comes Bob-Bob-Bobbin' Along." There were other songs my mother loved to hear me sing, like "Autumn Leaves" and "I Love Paris," but these selections would have been too evocative for a five-year-old to sing in kindergarten. I rehearsed every day, and my mother choreographed my movements and facial expressions to enhance the performance.

The day of the show was filled with bright sunshine and balmy breezes. I wore a bright red dress (inspired by the song), which was trimmed with a narrow border of white lace around the hem of the skirt, the collar, and the puffed short sleeves. My new white anklets also had lace trim and my Mary Janes sparkled as they reflected sunbeams (my mother swore the best thing for patent leather was a dab of Vaseline).

My mom and I walked to school together that afternoon, passing the shops that were already so familiar to me, like Sol's Delicatessen, where the grill inside the window was piled high with frankfurters and knishes. It was only two doors away from the Devon Movie Theatre where, as I got older, I would spend the best Saturday afternoons of my life watching double features, cartoons and a newsreel, all for twenty-five cents.

Next we passed the Daitch Dairy, which was owned and operated by Ann's parents. Here we would buy fresh pot cheese and cream cheese from a wooden carton. In the back was a large assortment of hard cheeses and olives, and other specialties. Up front were huge barrels of pickles. "A nickel for a pickle," we would say.

This became my favorite snack when I was older and walked home from school by myself. Soon we got to Norma's Card Shop, where my mother would buy my school supplies and sometimes coloring books and paper doll cutouts.

Crossing Tremont Avenue towards P.S. 28, I began to feel the butterflies flittering in my stomach. We kept going and finally felt the shade of those impressive columns and were admitted through the teacher's entrance. Slowly we climbed the wide staircase to the second floor. We entered the auditorium where we took our seats and I awaited my turn.

That room seemed so big to me.

There were rows and rows of attached wooden chairs with foldup seats, and each chair had a little numbered brass plaque screwed to its back. I watched and listened attentively as each child took a turn at performing on stage. The stage itself was beautiful. The back of it was arched in a semicircle, like a huge bay window.

It was made of panels of dark, polished mahogany, like the banister of the teacher's staircase, and it was very shiny. There was a tall, smooth, rounded column of the same polished wood on either end of the half-circle.

Set into those wooden panels were large, round plates of stained glass, which were dimly lit from behind. I was transfixed by the colors in those windows, and was to spend hundreds of Friday mornings in that auditorium, wearing my blue skirt, white blouse, and red sash, staring dreamily at that classic stage, watching a variety of presentations, always distracted by the beauty of the stained glass.

But now it was my turn. Somewhere between the ballerina and the baton twirler I was called up to sing about the Red Robin. I left my seat, walked down the aisle to the front, and up the two steps at the side of the stage. I focused on the clock on the back wall and never looked at anyone in the audience.

The accompanist gave me a signal on the piano and began to play, and I got through my two minutes or so without a hitch. I bowed politely as the appreciative applause ushered me back to my seat. My mother's hug was filled with approval and pride.

Later, on the way home, we stopped at Marty's Candy Store. I climbed onto one of the revolving stools at the counter, and my mom bought me an egg cream, fresh from the fountain, and a soft, chewy pretzel.

Then my mother and I held hands and walked the two blocks home to our apartment in an elevator building that featured dropped living rooms and casement windows.

Although there were other performances of one sort or another over the next twenty years or so of my life, this one is brightest in my memory and is the only one that I think of when I see or smell a fresh box of crayons.

Irene Gertrude Felix, 1921

Lydia Clark

Gertrude stretched trying to eradicate the uneasy feeling in her stomach. She hoped it was anticipation, or maybe it was the movement of the ocean, but she suspected it was the onset of that dreaded time of the month.

"Please, not now…not here," she said under her breath. Prayed silently to the saints in Spanish.

Gertrude did not want to go below deck to the berths and rummage through her belongings to retrieve "the rag". That meant she would have to use the bathroom and she knew none of the señoras who would accompany her to the bathroom, nor would she ask.

She wrinkled her nose at the thought of the horrible smell she would have to endure. The men that hung around the bathrooms watched her whenever she passed by and that made her uneasy. Why should they, the señoras, help?

They were not responsible for her. They had their own children to look out for and she was supposed to be sixteen years old anyway. She was a young señorita able to fend for herself and her brother, who was supposed to be fourteen and was only ten. Gertrude herself was only thirteen.

They were used to fending for themselves, and were encouraged to lie about their ages whenever it benefited them—and this was a big benefit. Gertrude thought about the big fiasco seven months ago in November when they first tried to make this trip. They were turned away because she and her brother gave their correct ages.

It was such a disappointment and lying about her age would become a habit that would plague her for the rest of her life.

Her stomach cramped again. Gertrude doubled over from the pain. "Lord give me strength!" she said.

The prayer she always heard mama saying, hoping it would work. Gertrude closed her eyes and tried to disassociate herself as she had done countless times before when faced with problems she had no control over.

Her thoughts rushed back to the day she was told by her aunties she was a woman. That was her first time, as far as her aunties were concerned. Gertrude had experienced her period way before they had figured it out. She thought she was sick or dying and secretly washed her panties in shame and fear and hung them outside her window at night so no one would know.

But one day her Aunt Nellie saw the stain on the back of her skirt and made a really big deal about it. She enlisted the help of her two elder sisters and proceeded to educate Gertrude about becoming a woman.

"Keep your rag clean and don't let me smell it, 'cause if I smell it, you can bet dogs smell it. And you don't want dogs chasin' you...do you?"

Her two other aunties nodded in unison, eyebrows raised, lips pursed. "You don't want no babies, either," one of them said, while both shook their heads, clucking their tongues.

Gertrude shook her head from side-to-side, wide eyed and overwhelmed, thoughts of babies and dogs chasing her. "I like dogs and I like babies," she said, but something told her to keep her thoughts silent.

With Gertrude forgotten, Nellie and the other aunts continued babbling on about dogs and babies, predicting Gertrude's future of having babies too soon and the illicit life she would lead if she didn't mind her elders. They continued with their cooking and cleaning and shaking their heads...family!

Gertrude opened her eyes and quickly scanned the deck of the ship *The Ponce*—grand, majestic, slowly making its way through the choppy waters to Ellis Island in the United States of America...to her mother. She was surprised that her eyes no longer watered at the thought of her mother, five years was a long time. A whole lot of living, good and bad, went into those years.

Gertrude spied her younger brother Pedro leaning on the ship's railing, talking to one of the ship's workers. She envied the way that her brother was always able to make friends wherever he went. He was very anxious to see this tall woman everyone was talking about—who would let them know they were near their destination, the United States of America.

A place, mama wrote, it was a good place...a place where there were opportunities and Gertrude and Pedro would attend school on a consistent basis and be with her all the time, with good living conditions in an apartment on East 116th Street.

There was a sudden shout and Gertrude looked in the direction of the commotion...

"There she is...there she is!"

A young man waved with excitement and pointed over the side. Everyone on deck moved to the side of the ship trying to see the magnificent lady. With all thoughts of pain forgotten, Gertrude jumped up to her feet to see for herself—pushing through the crowd of about eighty of her kinfolk from Puerto Rico.

She ran to her brother's side and gazed at the magnificent lady as they drew closer to her. They grabbed one another's hands and Gertrude's eyes filled with tears. Mama...

Trayectoría académica

José Cenac

El 5 de mayo del 2004 retomé mi educación universitaria ingresando a Essex County College en Newark, NJ. Finalmente me gradué con un Asociado en Ciencias de dicha institución académica el 3 de junio del 2007.

En enero del 2009 me matriculé en Lehman College empezando con una sola clase: Filosofía de la Religión. Mi experiencia en Lehman ha sido muy agradable, vigorizante y excitante hasta el momento de vivir una terrible experiencia con uno de mis profesores durante el semestre de otoño del 2010.

Tomé la iniciativa de matricularme por el semestre completo en el Centro Académico para la Excelencia (Academic Center for Excellence, ACE) para recibir tutoría en escritura y composición, exclusivamente para trabajar en las asignaciones de ensayos y diarios para el curso de educación ESC 409.

Mi primera sesión en el centro ACE fue el 5 de octubre, 2010 a las 9:00 a.m. El mismo día, a las 6:30 p.m., la clase de ESC 409 terminó, excepto para cinco estudiantes latinos—dominicanos, para ser especifico—quienes no estaban produciendo un trabajo aceptable en los ensayos y escrituras asignados.

Yo quedé solo en el aula con la profesora y su asistente. Le pregunté por mis ensayos previos para aprender de sus correcciones, comentarios, y observaciones.

—"No los tengo. Te sugiero que canceles esta clase porque no estás haciendo bien. No estás escribiendo a nivel universitario".

Le mostré prueba de asistencia a mi primera sesión de tutoría en el ACE, pero ella ni siquiera tomó un minuto para mirarla.

—"Estoy decidido a mejorar. Acabamos de empezar el semestre, sólo llevamos tres semanas. ¿Usted no confía en mí?"

—"Solamente sugerí que debes cancelar la clase".

—"No voy a cancelar la clase, y voy a pasar este curso".

—"Entonces, pruébame que estoy equivocada".

—"Ya sea que usted crea en mí o no, yo sé una cosa, confío en mí mismo, tengo la capacidad para cumplir con sus requisitos, y yo pasaré este curso. Su actitud negativa frente a mis esfuerzos y participación activa en clase me confirma lo que usted había dicho en la sesión donde discutíamos Las Inteligencias Múltiples de Howard Gardner: 'No tengo cualidades interpersonales'."

Esperaba que dijera algo como esto: "José, veo tu esfuerzo, veo tu activa participación en la clase. Veo que has tomado la iniciativa de matricularte en el centro ACE para las tutorías en escritura y composición de ensayos. Yo noté que tu escritura no llena mis requisitos, pero el semestre acaba de empezar. Trabaja duro, y continúa asistiendo a las sesiones de tutoría todas las semanas. Estoy segura que te pondrás al nivel requerido, y si me necesitas, yo estoy aquí para servirte. Yo confió en ti".

Este breve, poderoso, compasivo, empático y solidario pronunciamiento habría hecho una gran diferencia. Me sentí irrespetado y desconsiderado por su falta de compasión y empatía. Ella estaba tratando de matar mi esperanza. Tres semanas más tardes produje un ensayo grado "A".

Estaba esperando por ese ensayo semana tras semana para ver el grado, como un niño en espera impaciente para abrir sus regalos de Navidad.

La profesora terminó dándome un grado "F" al final del curso. Apelé, y el Comité de Apelación cambió el grado a una "C" sin proveerme una explicación de cómo ellos arribaron a ese grado final. Inmediatamente me di cuenta que era un grado político y diplomático, significando, le damos una "C" y él no tiene que retomar la clase, y el profesor no luce tan mal como si le diéramos lo que él se merece, por lo menos una "B+".

Mi experiencia educativa me recuerda a Richard Rodríguez, cuando él dijo en su autobiografía *Hunger of Memory*, "La confianza, la seguridad calmante de que yo pertenecía en público, finalmente se había afianzado".

Ese "pertenecer en público" es la habilidad de comunicarse en inglés propia y confortablemente. Todos los cursos que he tomado hasta ahora en mi experiencia universitaria han sido en inglés con excepción de los cursos en mi concentración de español. Ningún profesor me había dicho antes que yo no estaba escribiendo a nivel universitario.

Tuve dos experiencias diametralmente opuestas con dos profesores en el semestre de otoño 2010. La profesora descrita más arriba y la profesora de Burundi, África. Ella es empática, es interpersonal, es compasiva y es jovial. Ella también tiene un completo entendimiento de los diferentes orígenes de sus estudiantes, en otras palabras, tiene una gran sensibilidad hacia la diversidad cultural y racial de sus estudiantes.

En el futuro, yo imitaré su sensibilidad con mis propios estudiantes. Siempre recordaré estas dos profesoras, haciendo la distinción entre quien no tuvo una onza de relaciones interpersonales y quien fue la profesora de mayor empatía que haya tenido. Continuaré mejorando las habilidades y conocimientos en mi área y así como Maya Angelou nos invita a hacer, "Perseguiré las cosas que amo hacer, y las haré tan bien que la gente no me quitará los ojos de encima. Todas las otras tangibles recompensas vendrán como resultado".

Me aseguraré de ser recordado como el profesor más empático que mis estudiantes hayan tenido.

En mayo del 2012, me gradué Summa Cum Laude con una Licenciatura en Español y estudios de Educación. Dos años más tarde, el 29 de mayo del 2014 me gradué de nuevo Summa Cum Laude con una Maestría en Español.

El 22 de mayo, 2014, siete días antes de mi graduación, vi a mi profesora de Burundi. Cada vez que la veo, me alegra el día. Recuerdo que fui el único estudiante capaz de pronunciar su nombre completo tan pronto ella se presentó a los estudiantes.

Ella abrió esos ojotes llenos de vida y energía en absoluta sorpresa, cuando escuchó mi voz con un acento hispano pronunciando su nombre impecablemente: Inmaculée Harushimana.

Nosotros inmigramos a los Estados Unidos procedentes de países del Tercer Mundo: Burundi y la República Dominicana. Dos países tropicales localizados en diferentes continentes.

Una raíz: Madre África, "la cuna de la humanidad" esparcida por toda la faz de la tierra. Somos polvo estelar. Somos parte de todo lo que existe en el Universo. Estamos todos interconectados.

El Casi-casi esta vez en mayo

Jhon Sánchez

Todavía le sigo viendo pero esta vez como un fantasma que se desaparece entre las multitudes de Fordham Road. Esa calle del Bronx en que los vientos de los sábados y los domingos parecen esparcir una polvoreada de gentes; sin embargo le he visto a él, el casi-amigo, el casi-novio, el nunca-nada que bailaba apretado de cadera a cadera, a mi cadera; aquel que leía su presencia en mis poemas.

En la esquina de Conway le veo con la mirada hacia el cielo y las manos en los bolsillos. A la vuelta, en Grand Concourse, está su "shelter". Pienso que es posible que hubiese regresado a la prostitución. Espero que no. Pero si está allí congelado en una esquina como si fuese parte de una carambola del destino a la cual me voy a estrellar.

Mi corazón se desemboca, giro hacia la izquierda, y encuentro que la luz del semáforo está a punto de cambiar. Alcanzo a huir. En la esquina miro de reojo. Él no está allí. Se ha esfumado y me pregunto, ¿"Hacia dónde?"

Se ha ocultado con el sigilo de primate con el cual se saltaba sobre mis sabanas. Al despertar era como si él nunca hubiese existido; y para probarme mi propia sanidad mental, asumía el papel de arqueólogo que tuviese que conjeturar la veracidad de ese cuerpo en un espacio cóncavo debajo de las cobijas.

En esa esquina de Fordham Road parece como si la multitud de los cuerpos se interceptaran díscolos dejando solo un punto del tamaño de eso pies delgados, morenos, que bailan capoeira y que se envuelven en vendajes el dolor de una artritis.

¿'Estaría esperando un 'user'?'

No quiero que regrese a la prostitución. Él me señaló los sitios donde sus clientes lo recogían, donde esperó su primer contrato de pornografía, allá debajo del tren 2, Simpson Avenue. Al caminar a su lado, los edificios antiguos ocultaban en sus apartamentos historias de sex-parties y los árboles guardaban en sus raíces los condones, que si acaso, dejó usados.

"Prostitución no es una opción para un hijo." Dije en una cena. Mi frase tenía el nombre y apellido de mi casi-amante, casi-amigo, casi-casi si le podría llamar así a quien vivió conmigo por dos años.

Me muevo esquivando los transeúntes, parece que voy en la dirección contraria y todos viniesen de Grand Concourse. Recuerdo que la semana pasada era el día de la madre. Me bajé en Burnside para encontrarme con un hombre Afro, no tan alto pero torneado.

Le había conocido en el tren y mostró curiosidad infantil por mi celular. He descifrado de su inglés entre dientes que había estado 18 años preso. Le aconsejé que tomara unas clases de computadoras, 'First;' al mismo tiempo le acaricié sus bíceps.

En Burnside, sus ojos parecían centrados en mi cuerpo delgado. Encontré su barbilla sin rasurar tentadora. Sus labios babeaban pero sus ojos me rehusaban. Me explicó que tenía que llevar un ramo de flores a su ex-mujer, "My daughter's mother."

El sol picaba y yo le esperé en un cuchifrito. Yolanda, una dominicana, me había servido un jugo de parchita. No vi que puso el pitillo.

Le pregunté por él y ella me responde, "No me digas que puede chupar dos al mismo tiempo."

Y lanzó una mirada donde El Afro, ahora rasurado, me esperaba. Me había estado mirando por un rato.

Una vez me acerco él, sin preámbulos me invita a un parque. "No! Estoy dispuesto a pagar un hotel," le dije.

Él me ha respondido que hay uno en Grand Concourse. Caminé hacia allá para hacer la reservación y esperar su llamada.

Vi el letrero de 'hotel' y entré. Pregunté con la mirada baja, "Short terms?" No sé cómo se diría en español.

"No," me responde un hombre hispano con cabello indio y bigote. Él leyó la extrañeza en mi rostro, "No, eso no funciona aquí. Esto es un shelter del gobierno."

De inmediato me di cuenta que mi casi-amante, mi casi-amigo, el casi-nada, el casi-casi, podía estar allí. Salí del 'hotel' apresuradamente. Si me hubiese visto, me acusaría de estar persiguiéndole.

El teléfono timbró, era el Afro. Lo imaginé al borde de la cama desnudo después de hacer el amor. Se había sentado a recontarme la historia de que no tiene trabajo. Sé bien que tengo que esculcar en mis bolsillos por un billete que valga el día de la madre. Sin amenaza, sin un pacto antes de, sin ser prostitución pero ante mi propio miedo sé que esto tiene un precio.

El teléfono siguió timbrando. Borré mis besos imaginarios con el Afro. Y de manera inusitada me entré a un Delgado Travel. Sentado en una silla plástica blanca había un hombre puertorriqueño, grueso y de bigote. Tenía una rosa marchita en la mano izquierda y la palma derecha extendida, musitando entre dientes, "Una quarter. Tengo hambre."

Con recriminación y perfecta articulación me recordó, "It is Mother's Day."

Hice la fila y apagué el teléfono, ya que para el momento tenía tres llamadas perdidas del Afro. Desde las cabinas telefónicas una mejicana le decía a su hijo que a los pantalones que le mandó, "le puede coger el dobladillo."

La fila avanzó de dos en dos; pues en parejas se acercaban a la ventanilla donde una mujer cuenta los fajos de billetes que van a Cuenca, Guadalajara, o Santo Domingo. Probablemente porque no vio un fajo de billetes en mis manos, la cajera me preguntó, "Va a llamar a su mamá?"

Al sentir ese acento paisa imaginé el rostro de mi mamá adornado con corazones peruanos en un ataúd que nunca vi. Decidí mentir. "Quiero viajar a Colombia y deseo saber el costo de los tiquetes."

Pero no era una mentira porque si pudiese hacer ese viaje, El Bronx desaparecería de mí, llevándose a ese casi-amigo, casi amante, casi-casi quien abandonó las llaves de mi apartamento al lado de un calendario de mariposas del 2014.

Made in the USA
Middletown, DE
25 February 2015